THE
FROM THE
PHILOKALIA

Number 1:
WATCHFULNESS
AND PRAYER

by

Archimandrite IOANNIKIOS

*　　*　　*

Translated from the Greek
by
Jeannie E. Gentithes and
Archim. Ignatios Apostolopoulos

With an Introduction by
Father JOHN CHAKOS

Light and Life Publishing Company
Minneapolis, Minnesota

i

Light and Life Publishing Company
P.O. Box 26421
Minneapolis, Minnesota 55426-0421

Copyright © 1988
Jeannie E. Gentithes
Library of Congress Card No. 88-82958

ISBN 0-937032-59X

DEDICATION

To our spiritual Father,
Archimandrite EPHRAIM,
Abbot of the Holy Monastery of Philotheou,
without whose blessing this book
would not have been possible.

CONTENTS

PREFACE

"The study of divine principles teaches knowledge of God to the person who lives in truth, longing and reverence."[1] "Knock, and it will be opened to you."[2] The pious study of the Sacred Scriptures leads to opening the door of divine knowledge, to revelation of ineffable mysteries, to a purified heart burning with heavenly longing and divine eros for the Kingdom of God and eternal life: "This is eternal life, that they know Thee the only true God, and Jesus Christ Whom Thou hast sent."[3]

In the contemporary rabble of human opinions and false knowledge, in the flood of human words and philosophies, "blessed is the man who . . . on the law of the Lord . . . meditates day and night."[4]

The Philokalia is a true "neptic" encyclopedia, i.e., an encyclopedia of watchfulness, study and commentary of Holy Scripture, and of the Mystical Orthodox Tradition; it is a philosophy of action in Christ the God-Man; it is the road leading man to his divine destiny, to deification by grace, and to contemplation through asceticism; it is a collection of powerful texts, the fruit of Orthodox spirituality. They are offered here in fragments from the classic work, The Philokalia.

Our Orthodox Church is the Church of the Fathers, of watchfulness, of asceticism, of the Philokalia. The "neptic" hue of the Philokalia permeates the Church in all its expressions and arts. An effort is made here to recover this purely Orthodox color (like the marvelous Byzantine fresco which has been painted over and covered by a fleshy, rationalistic, European painting of western origin). The THEMES FROM THE PHILOKALIA must uncover it within Holy Scripture, the lives of our saints, the apophthegmata of the ascetics, the texts of the Fathers, our Hymnology, our Liturgy, our contemporary ascetic scene. Besides, the depth of Orthodox life according to the Fathers of the Philokalia is not new: it is the very essence of the everlasting, inviolate and unchanging Tradition of our Church.

1

THEMES FROM THE PHILOKALIA are intended mainly for the average layman. They seek to contribute to the knowledge of the mystical life of our Church to the general public. Especially in our times, the thirst for such a pure fountain becomes stronger in fellow Orthodox as well as in the heterodox and followers of Eastern religions drowning in the sea of an egocentric or demonic mysticism. Only Orthodox mysticism is Life, Grace, Joy, Light, and Truth.

THEMES FROM THE PHILOKALIA will comprise a series of separate volumes readily accessible and easy to comprehend. We present here the first volume in the series, titled "Watchfulness and Prayer."

It is our hope that spiritual progress in watchfulness, coupled with frequent sacramental and eucharistic life, will help essentially our shepherds and their flock with their spiritual renewal in Christ during these difficult, arid, and unproductive years.

Whatever these THEMES have to say is not the property of the "poor and needy"[5] author. Their content is but a loan from the inexhaustible spiritual Treasury of the holy Fathers and from the inheritance they left to us, their modern, unwise children; an inheritance which up to now has remained untouched on the dusty shelves of our libraries. . . . They have only this to say, only this message to send:

". . . It is full time now for you to wake from sleep."[6]
It is time for repentance and joyful mourning.
It is time for watchfulness and prayer.

INTRODUCTION:
JOURNEY TO THE
KINGDOM WITHIN

A man saw his friend searching for something on the ground. "What have you lost, my brother?" he asked.

"My key," said the man.

So his friend went down on his knees too, and they both looked for it. After a time, the other man asked: "Where exactly did you drop it?"

"In my own house."

"Then why are you looking here?"

"There is more light here than inside my own house."

This little story is a parable of modern life. We look for insight and understanding into the nature of things, we search for meaning and direction to life, we desire communion with God, but we go on searching in the wrong places. The light in our parable corresponds to the intellectual approach to life. The darkness has to do more with the heart, the spirit, the inner life of a person. As people who are strongly influenced by a culture that places a premium on rational thought, we are faced with a dilemma when it comes to God. In order to find Him, we have to let go of intellect, of reason, of the ego, and enter the darkness of our innermost self. St. Isaac the Syrian, that great mystic of our Church, puts it this way: "Make peace with yourself, and heaven and earth will make peace with you. Take pains to enter your own innermost chamber and you will see the chamber of heaven, for they are one and the same, and in entering one you behold them both."

This then is the task for every Orthodox Christian. We are to enter the innermost chamber of the self, sometimes called the heart, and there we are to look for "the deposit of grace," the buried talent, given to us in Baptism. The gift has not been destroyed, but only buried as a treasure in the ground of our hearts. If we truly desire to find what the Lord has given to us in

3

Baptism, then we must diligently search to unearth this treasure of the heart and bring it to light. This can be done in two ways. In the words of St. Gregory of Sinai, "the gift of Baptism is revealed first of all by a painstaking fulfillment of the commandments ('If you love me you will keep my commandments[7]'). The more we carry these out, the more clearly the gift shines upon us in its brilliance. Secondly, it comes to light and is revealed through the continual remembrance of God in prayer."

We will refer to the first method as the outer journey and in itself it is very powerful. But the second method is more so, giving strength to our fidelity to the commandments. For this reason we should hasten to make the inner journey to God's Kingdom. Let us focus our attention on this inner journey to the kingdom within, why we must make it, how it is made and what treasure it produces.

WHY MUST WE MAKE THE INNER JOURNEY? The essence of the Christian life has more to do with the inner life of the soul than with external conduct. Unless we plunge into the depths of our being through the doorway of repentance, fidelity to the commandments by itself cannot save us. St. Theophan the Recluse in the Anthology *The Art of Prayer* teaches that "people concern themselves with Christian upbringing but leave it incomplete; they neglect the most essential and most difficult side of the Christian life, and dwell on what is easiest, the visible and external." We have to be wary of observing with the utmost correctness all the formal and outward rules for devout conduct, while neglecting the inner life of the soul. We all know what it means to be "pharisaic" in the practice of our faith. Theophan reminds us that this approach to the spiritual life results in a lack of inner peace. In essence what Theophan is saying is that we must address ourselves to the needs of the whole person and not just a single part.

Theophan goes on to say that "without inner spiritual prayer, there is no prayer at all, for this alone is real prayer, pleasing to God." At times we are all guilty of being parrots when we pray. We glibly mouth the words, but our hearts and minds are a thousand miles away. When inner prayer is absent, the words have only the appearance and not the reality of prayer. Are there not certain prayers that all of us have come to say in an automatic way? We go through all the motions of prayer, but our hearts and minds are not in it. The Lord's Prayer, for example, is one that we most commonly abuse in this way. We can actually recite the words and be thinking of something completely unrelated. This double-minded approach to prayer must be avoided at all costs. The essence of prayer has been properly described by Theophan as "the spiritual lifting of the heart towards God."

Surely, one of the most profound statements ever made about inner prayer was given to us by Isaac the Syrian: "Enter eagerly into the treasure-house that lies within you, and so you will see the treasure-house of heaven; for the two are the same, and there is but one single entry to them both. The ladder that leads to the Kingdom is hidden within you, and is found in your soul. Dive into yourself and in your soul and you will discover the rungs by which to ascend." What a profound mystery this prayer journey into inner space becomes! As we descend into the depths of our being, we ascend to the heights of heaven. Have we not all, at one time or another, ascended the ladder to heaven during some privileged moment of deep inner prayer or worship? The Divine Liturgy calls us to many such moments: "Let us lift up our hearts — We lift them up unto the Lord."

Theophan describes this ascent to inner spiritual prayer as evolving in three phases. The first degree is *bodily prayer,* which consists for the most part of reading, standing and making prostrations. With this form of prayer, the heart initially feels nothing and has no desire to pray. On Mt. Athos the young monks are instructed to begin reciting the Jesus Prayer out loud, even while engaging in other activities. After a while the bodily prayer in this case moves from the lips into the mind, thus becoming *mental prayer,* or as Theophan calls it, "prayer with attention." At this stage of prayer, we begin focusing the mind on the words of prayer, making the words our own. Of course, as we attempt to pray in this way, many distracting thoughts will disturb our focus. The phenomenon of instant replay will bring to mind a host of troubling emotions, conflicts, fears and anxieties. The muddied waters of an active life rise up to quench our prayer of attention, but we must discipline ourselves to remain silent. The third degree

5

that Theophan speaks of is "the prayer of feeling," when the heart itself is warmed by a feeling that results in continuous contrition. What before was a pious thought now becomes a feeling. A contrite phrase becomes contrition itself. In a sense we are taken over by the prayer. We no longer recite prayer, we are prayer.

When this sense of being taken over by prayer occurs, real prayer may be said to begin. "The spiritual realm opens up to us and we are granted the vision of another world," to use the words of Theophan. God taps us on the shoulder with this call of deeper prayer, now we must respond to it. God has done His part, now we must give Him resounding our "Yes." From this point on we must work to keep ourselves in this state of grace. Many good beginnings in prayer have come to naught for lack of a commitment to this deeper way of life. Many of us stop here. We are afraid to make the inner journey to this kingdom.

But for those who wish to continue, the next question that arises is: HOW DO WE MAKE THE INNER JOURNEY? Regarding the inner journey, Theophan prefaces his teaching with a paradoxical statement. He tells us that we will achieve nothing by our own efforts; yet God will not give us anything, unless we work with all our strength. Remember the pilgrim in *The Way of the Pilgrim?* He was told to give the quantity and God would provide the quality. It's like trying to start a fire by rubbing two pieces of wood together. If we don't rub, the fire won't start. Yet at precisely what moment the fire comes, we can't say. Think of the dancer who tries to master a certain routine. She rehearses it over and over again, until one day it comes effortlessly. The dance and the dancer become one. Listen to this testimony cited by Theophan about a man from Kiev who said: "I did not use any methods at all, I did not know the Jesus prayer, yet by God's mercy I walk always in His presence. But how this has come to pass, I myself do not know. God gave!" Real prayer, we must realize, is always God-given; otherwise we may confuse the gift of grace with some achievement of our own.

About the methodology of prayer, Theophan teaches that God is pleased by two forms of prayer, that written by others and our own prayers. Only prayer said in a perfunctory manner is displeasing to God. With any prayer that is read, however, we must make it our own. Also, it is not enough just to wait for the desire to pray. To achieve spontaneous prayer, we must force ourselves to pray, even when we don't feel like it. Every Orthodox Christian should have his or her own prayer rule, that is, a set time for prayer. This discipline should be adhered to faithfully.

To assist us in our spiritual journey, we must all enlist the services of a spiritual guide, one who is experienced in the spiritual life and faithfully follow his or her counsel to us. As the Fathers so often remind us, we can do nothing by ourselves. The pitfalls are many for those who would make the inward journey. Spiritual pride is particularly dangerous. For this reason the Desert Christians teach, "If you see a young monk climbing up to heaven by his own will, grasp him by the feet and throw him down, for this is to his profit. . . ." St. Anthony confirms the wisdom of this saying with these words: "So far as possible, for every step that a monk takes, for every drop of water that he drinks in his cell, he should entrust the decision to the Old Men, to avoid making some mistake in what he does." We must never doubt that at the very moment we begin praying, our adversary the devil will seek every possible avenue open to him to bring us down. Our spiritual guide must be there to help us over the high and low points of the journey. Self-stripping through obedience to another is the Orthodox way.

As to the length of prayer, St. Dimitri Rostov teaches that "prayer should be short but oft repeated." In this way, the mind will not be distracted in a search for words, as St. John of the Ladder instructs us. [8] The shorter prayers allow the mind to focus itself. The faithful repetition of the Jesus prayer allows us to concentrate on the deeper reality that it conveys. After all, the purpose of all prayer is to place us in the presence of God. We must go beyond the words to the reality. Simple prayer, like the Jesus prayer, facilitates this process. It takes us a step beyond reason. We can let go. It makes it easier for us to contain the wandering of the mind. On Mt. Athos, for example, the Jesus prayer is reduced to five words in Greek. "Lord Jesus Christ / have mercy / on me."

7

Besides short prayers, Theophan teaches that psalms, hymns and church songs can help in achieving the state of inner prayer. He writes: "The Spirit of God filled His elect, and they expressed the plenitude of their feelings in songs. He who sings them as they should be sung enters again into the feelings which the author experienced when he originally wrote them." Let's take the Liturgy as an example of what Theophan is talking about. In the beginning we feel a dryness. The service is not alive for us. As we focus on the prayers, hymns and petitions, however, we have a change of heart. What before seemed dry and boring comes alive. The spark of baptismal grace that is hidden within us burns brighter and with greater warmth. In the words of Theophan, "Psalms, hymns and spiritual odes . . . fan the spark and transform it into flame." He likens this action to the wind igniting a spark hidden in firewood.

Theophan speaks again about this spark of grace in connection with the Jesus prayer. He teaches that "when God's spark falls into the heart, the Jesus prayer fans it into flame." He's quick to point out that the prayer itself does not produce the spark, but only prepares the way for it. When the fire of grace appears in the heart, then it is possible for self-acting or infused prayer to begin.

The attitude that we have when praying is also a precondition for its ultimate success. Theophan instructs us to "stand before God in reverence and fear, with the mind in the heart." He goes on to say that "these feelings of fear and sorrow in the sight of God, the broken and contrite heart, are the principle features of true inner prayer. . . ." At this point we must issue a warning when these feelings are absent. Spiritual pride and delusion are real dangers of the spiritual life. Many have fallen thinking that they are spiritually advanced. When in doubt as to the disposition of our prayer life, we must consult with our spiritual guide.

One last thing with regard to the methodology of prayer that must be emphasized. No progress can be made without suffering. To pray in this deeper way is a struggle, a struggle against distraction, against temptation, against our tendency to be lax regarding spiritual endeavor. In the words of Theophan, "He who proceeds without suffering will bear no fruit." Those who are condemned for spiritual fruitlessness will hear the words, "Take the talent from him."[9] We are reminded in Scripture that "the kingdom of heaven suffers violence, and the violent take it by force."[10] "Via, via" is an often repeated phrase on Mt. Athos, that is "be forceful with yourself." In America don't we say, "No pain, no gain"?

WHAT ARE THE TREASURES THAT WE CAN UNEARTH THROUGH THIS TYPE OF INNER PRAYER? A woman who began in earnest to use the Jesus Prayer expected more from it than she appeared to receive. She went to her spiritual father and inquired of him, "Why do I feel nothing when I pray?" In her mind the fruits of prayer should be joy, ecstasy and beatitude. Instead of these exalted states she was only feeling remorse over her sinfulness. St. Theophan's answer is very illuminating for all of us: "The principal fruit of prayer is not warmth and sweetness, but fear of God and contrition." In our spiritual infancy, we look for Taborian experiences when we pray. We become easily disappointed when nothing seems to happen. We question the efficacy of our prayer. But Theophan reminds us that what we seek in prayer is to establish in our hearts a quiet but warm and constant feeling towards God. He is quick to add, though, that when God does give us a mountaintop experience in prayer, we must be grateful for it and not imagine that it is due to ourselves. Nor are we to be dismayed when the ecstasy leaves us.

To help us put things in a little better perspective when it comes to ecstatic states, the following anecdote may be helpful. A certain pious woman described the method she used to get her dog into the basement. She would take a piece of meat, lead him to the top of the steps, then throw it down the basement for him to retrieve. Ecstatic states of prayer, when they do come, often are a preparation for some new challenge to our lives. Strengthened by the moment on the mountain, we have to descend into the valley of life's problems. It might be that a cross is waiting for us.

Theophan enjoins us to practice the prayer in simplicity, with our attention in the heart, always holding on to the remembrance of God. This concentration results in the centering of the mind, "devoutness and fear of God, recollection of death and stillness of

9

thought, and a certain warmth of heart." Theophan calls these "natural fruits" of prayer in the heart, and not the fruit of grace. He tells us this lest we become boastful about what is happening. Only when grace comes, Theophan teaches, can prayer be said to begin. "The coming of grace," he adds, "is the sign that God has looked on us in mercy."

One thing that Theophan will not do, however, is to describe what happens when grace does come. Like most of the Fathers and Mothers of the Church, Theophan maintains a pious silence on this point. Their only answer seems to be, "When grace comes you will know it."

In Baptism and Chrismation, then, we all received the gift of grace. According to this we should therefore burn in our spirit, which is animated by the Holy Spirit. Why is it, then, that we are not alive with baptismal fervor? We have buried the "deposit of grace." Preoccupation with worldly affairs can overwhelm a fledgling inner life. In order to unearth this treasure and fan the spark of grace into flame, we must reorder our priorities, orienting our lives towards the contemplation of what is divine, holy, heavenly and eternal. We must first begin by obeying all the commandments of God. Then, with the name of Jesus on our lips and in our minds, we must plunge into the depths of our being seeking the buried talent. When we have applied ourselves to this work with patience and humility, God in His mercy will envelope us with His love. We will also discover a new spiritual world of unsurpassed beauty and calm, a world where Jesus Christ reigns in our hearts forever.

Father John Chakos

10

PROLOGUE

Watchfulness in ecclesiastical terminology means wakefulness, fine and unceasing vigilance of the mind and heart. It is also known as attentiveness, or guarding of the intellect. The noun "watchfulness" is derived from the verb "to watch," which signifies: "I am careful, wakeful, alert, sober."

In order for watchfulness to bear fruit, it must be coupled with prayer, particularly with the mental, unceasing prayer of the heart. One cannot conceive of watchfulness without mental prayer and, conversely, mental prayer without watchfulness. The two are inseparable in the work of the purification of the heart from passions, in the unseen warfare with the unclean thoughts and demons.

Watchfulness and mental prayer is not the exclusive property of monastics. To be sure, it is used primarily by them because their quiet, saintly life renders itself to it more readily. However, if it is every man's destiny to be deified through purification from passions — and without this internal catharsis, in the words of the Lord,[11] everything else is futile — then watchfulness and prayer open the age-old tried and tested road which leads to the perfection described in the Gospels.

Therefore, whoever of our readers, monastics or laymen, wants to follow the road of Elijah the Tishbite; whoever is aflame with the desire to become a "second herald of Christ," a desire generated inside us by the prayer of the heart; let him prepare the chariot of watchfulness and prayer in order to ride heavenward with the zealous prophet.

St. Hesychios the Presbyter has these wise words to say: "A true monk is one who has achieved watchfulness; and he who is truly watchful is a monk in his heart."[12] We believe that the saint will justify us if we generalize this truth — something which the Holy Scripture and Sacred Tradition of our Church confirm — and say: "A true Christian is one who achieves watchfulness; and he who is truly watchful is a Christian at heart."

11

WATCHFULNESS
IN THE
HOLY SCRIPTURE

We said that watchfulness and vigilance in thoughts, in feelings, and in our heart is the work of all Christians, and Holy Scripture itself has become the first source of inspiration and valuation of watchfulness. And Holy Scripture does not address monastics only. It addresses all Christians. If watchfulness be the lot of the monastics-ascetics because of the conditions of the physical and spiritual environment in which they live, it is equally true that the faithful, within their capabilities, cannot be left without their share in regard to watchful life and its gifts, because a watchful life is nothing more than a life of incessant struggle, a life of contrition and joyful sadness, a life of wrestling with passions and purification, love and theosis.

Numerous are the passages which tell us about watchfulness, thus securing it scripturally. We shall refer to a few selectively.

There is a passage in the Old Testament which is a true neptic treasure: "Take heed to thyself that there be not a secret thing in thine heart, an iniquity. . . ."[13] Attention to yourself, fathoming inside the abyss of your heart to the extreme limits of your conscious or unconscious personality is the manifestation, practice and dimension of watchfulness: "Take heed to thyself. . . ."

In Proverbs 4:23[14] the divinely inspired author writes: "Keep your heart with all vigilance."

In the 25th chapter of the Gospel according to Matthew, the Lord narrates the very delightful but also painful parable of the ten virgins. Who really doubts that parable as being one of watchfulness, spiritual wakening and ever-readiness of the bride-soul? Could it be that with this story Christ wanted to stress to us the readiness of the mind, the uninterrupted and awakening of the heart; that is, its watchfulness inside the frightful night of passions and the quick darkness of the world outside and inside us? Could it be that Christ, the Divine Bridegroom, wanted to characterize the guarding of watchfulness as true wisdom and its loss as foolishness?

The five wise Virgins had oil in their lamps, the oil of love, and they had light, the light of watchfulness and prayer. The five foolish ones had neither one nor the other. For indeed love and watchful prayer are united together and compose a worthy preparation for the Bridegroom. But even with ardent, spontaneous, existential love with "all one's soul, heart and strength," perfect love toward Christ and toward one's neighbor-brother, you still cannot have the light of watchfulness and prayer. Yet without that Light you do not know where you are, where you are walking, where you are heading, you cannot even see your own self, nor your brother, nor the demons, not even the Bridegroom Himself Who comes "to the marriage feast." When love lessens, watchfulness and prayer lessen. When love is extinguished, watchfulness and prayer are extinguished. Still without watchfulness and prayer you cannot always keep your lamp filled with the oil of love.

Behold the sweetest end of the work of watchfulness and love: "The Bridegroom came, and those who were ready went in with Him to the marriage feast."[15] And the awful end of negligence: "Afterward the other virgins came also saying, 'Lord, Lord, open to us.' But He replied and said, 'Truly I say to you, I do not know you.'"[16]

Let us hear the analysis that St. Mark the Ascetic makes for us on this in the Philokalia:[17]

". . . The foolish virgins did indeed preserve their outer virginity, yet in spite of this were not admitted to the marriage-feast; they also had some oil in their vessels, that is, they possessed some virtues and external achievements and some gifts of grace, so that their lamps remained alight for a certain time. But because of negligence, ignorance and laziness they were not provident, and did not pay careful attention to the hidden swarm of passions energized within them by the evil spirits. Their thoughts were corrupted by . . . this demonic activity and shared in it. They were secretly enticed and overcome by malicious envy, by jealousy that hates everything good, by strife, quarreling, hatred, anger, bitterness, rancor, hypocrisy, wrath, pride, self-esteem, love of popu-

13

larity, self-satisfaction, avarice, listlessness, by sensual desire which provokes images of self-indulgence, by unbelief, irreverence, cowardice, dejection, contentiousness, sluggishness, sleep, presumption, self-justification, pomposity, boastfulness, insatiateness, profligacy, greed, by despair which is the most dangerous of all. . . .

"Thus they were deprived of the joy of the Bridegroom and shut out from the heavenly bridal chamber. Pondering, assessing and testing all this, let us realize our situation and correct our way of life. . . . Therefore, my son, he who wishes to take up the cross and follow Christ must first acquire spiritual knowledge and understanding **through constantly examining his thoughts,** showing the utmost concern for his salvation, and seeking God with all his strength . . . so that he does not travel in the dark without a light, not knowing how or where to walk."

The conclusion of the parable is nothing more than a commendation of the Lord for watchfulness and wakefulness. **"Watch** therefore, for you know neither the day nor the hour wherein the Son of man comes."[18]

In Mark 13:33, with the same thought in mind, He says: **"Take heed, watch** and pray." What impresses one is the first one, which in the Greek not only means "take heed," but also "look." Rightfully, then, did the holy Fathers name watchfulness the vision and the eye of the soul.

In Luke 21:34, having foretold the fearsome events of His Second Coming, the Lord underlines a serious danger, that of our hearts "being weighed down." And our hearts are "weighed down" by many and different causes. What can redeem them from that disastrous evil? Christ's commendation: "Take heed to yourselves," the attention, that is, the watchfulness which the Lord stresses in other words further down: **"Watch** therefore at all times praying. . . ."[19]

"At all times." The mind and heart must keep their vigilant guard every moment and every hour, day and night. And especially "praying." He links watchfulness and prayer.

14

The Lord shows us the same connection and the same unity of watchfulness and prayer on the night of His betrayal, when during those agonizing moments at Gethsemane after His stirring prayer, soaked in sweat and blood, He found His disciples sleeping. **"Keep awake** and **pray,"** He told them, ''that you may not enter into temptation.''[20] In other words, wakefulness means watchfulness and "to wake" is "to watch."

"To this day the agony of Gethsemane hosts sleeping Christians with bitterness," writes Professor J. Kornarakis. "Still today their role is one of compunction and wakefulness during the most crucial hour, the eleventh hour of Jesus' agony. It is to these sleeping Christians, that is, to us, that His piercing question is addressed: 'Could you not watch with Me one hour?'[21]

"What a pity! The thought and gaze of Jesus of Gethsemane can find rest only in neptic lives. . . . The technological Christian sleeps through the existential agony of his time, bringing him defenseless to the twelfth hour of the Judgement! . . ."

All the strategy of mental and unseen warfare is condensed within this phrase of the Lord: "Watch and pray, that you enter not into temptation."

The Apostle Paul, among others, in I Thessalonians 5:1 - 8, writes about the sudden day of Christ's coming as resembling a thief in the night, with Christians being "the sons of light and the sons of the day," and concludes: "So then let us not sleep, as others do, but let us **keep awake** and **be sober.** For those who sleep sleep at night, and those who get drunk are drunk at night. But since we belong to the day, let us **be sober,** and put on the breastplate of faith and love, and for a helmet the hope of salvation."

In that apostolic excerpt we can observe three noteworthy characteristics: Our mind and in general our entire inner man watches when he is awake, when he lives in the light of day, which is the life of Christ.

Night is for sleeping and drunkards. Lack of watchfulness brings sleep and "weighing down" of the heart, and drunkenness, which comes from worldly cares, filthy thoughts and passions.

15

Watchfulness further dresses the fighter with the armor of the Spirit, without which he is doomed in the mental unseen warfare.

The Apostle Paul, giving his fatherly and apostolic heritage to his disciple Timothy in II Timothy 4:5, tells him among other things: ". . . As for you, **watch** in all things."

In the First Catholic Epistle of Peter 1:13, we read a passage with unique and rare reference to the work of watchfulness: "Therefore gird up your minds, **be sober,** set your hope fully upon the grace that is coming to you at the revelation of Jesus Christ." All of the Holy Fathers agree that watchfulness and mental prayer bestow the Grace of the Holy Spirit and give to the soul the revelation of Christ, Who, without prayer and watchfulness, remains hidden. . . .

In 4:7 of the same Epistle the Apostle again entreats and exhorts Christians: "Be therefore sober and **watch** unto prayer."

To be sure, all the Apostles knew the value of watchfulness but experienced it negatively, having fallen into the temptation of the scandal and abandonment of the Teacher. But it seems the Apostle Peter experienced it more than the others; he, who in spite of all his enthusiasm and promises, succumbed to the temptation of denial.

If the Apostle Peter had greater watchfulness, attention, and prayer, perhaps he would not have denied the Lord in those tragic moments of his dilemma in the high priest's courtyard. Watchfulness and prayer would have dispersed his cowardice, given him the courage of confession, and strengthened his love toward the Lord. Temptation found the heart unguarded: it appeared, invaded, imprisoned the consent, and conquered him. Fortunately not for long, permanently, or decisively. The inner world of his soul alerted him: he awakened, regained his watchful armor, and Peter "went out and wept bitterly."

Because of this painful experience, he stresses watchfulness and its beneficial results three times in only one of his Catholic epistles, the first one.

In I Peter 5:8 he gives us a very expressive, vivid picture of the enemy of souls, the devil. He compares him to a wild lion that

16

roars, that prowls, looking to the right and to the left, seeking someone to devour. Full of hatred, envy, and malice. Tireless, very cunning, ingenious, soul-destroying. In this description the devil appears as a never-sleeping beast, a sly spirit full of watchfulness for infernal action and destruction! His indefatigable work is filth, confusion, the scattering and grazing of the mind and heart to things base and servile, the thwarting of the blissful union of the soul with its Life and Light.

In this unceasing, persisting, and endless hunt of the devil, the inspired word of God through the Apostle's mouth tells us: **"Be sober, be watchful.** Your adversary the devil prowls around like a roaring lion, seeking someone to devour."

*   *   *

We could say that the Lord's entire Sermon on the Mount[22] is a neptic homily where our Theanthropic Savior pinpoints for us the root of the passions, but at the same time He also plants the root of the true spiritual life. This is where the work of watchfulness is to be found: where the finest pulsations of the heart are, the beats which move and direct everything: thoughts and words, and memories, feelings, actions, and deeds.

Here is an example: Both purity and adultery start from the heart. There is spiritual adultery and carnal adultery, and the first may exist without the second. The Lord wants to cleanse our hearts from every passionate moment (desire) which brings adultery to the heart. "I say to you that everyone who looks at a woman lustfully has already committed adultery with her in his heart."[23]

We see that the Lord characterizes the heart as the source and root and mother and beginning of all carnal and spiritual fruit, as much in the Sermon on the Mount as in His teaching generally.

"If your eye be single, your whole body will be full of light; but if your eye be evil, your whole body will be full of darkness."[24] Let us see how St. Gregory Palamas speaks about the root of the passions and purification:

17

"Although passions exist in children by nature — even before their intellect becomes impassioned — they do not cooperate with them in the commission of a sin but for the formation of their nature. That is why they are not wicked. Therefore, since carnal passions get their start from an impassioned intellect, we must start the therapy from there. As in a fire, he who volunteers to put it out, if he cuts the flame from on high, has not succeeded in anything. If, however, he removes the matter of the fire, the fire goes out at once. This happens with carnal passions also.

"If you do not dry out the source of thoughts with prayer and humility and arm yourself against them solely with fasting and physical hardship, you labor in vain. If, however, you sanctify the root with humility and prayer, as we said, you will also have sanctified the external senses."[25]

Filthy heart, filthy flesh. Clean heart, clean flesh. Impassioned heart, impassioned body. Dispassionate heart, dispassionate body. . . . "Hypocrites! for you cleanse the outside of the cup and of the plate, but inside they are full of extortion and rapacity. You blind Pharisee! first cleanse the inside of the cup and of the plate, that the outside also may be clean."[26] That is the cleanliness the Lord wants.

The heart is a workshop, a noiseless and silent workshop where its fruits have immeasurable strength, "nuclear" energy: either demonic and destructive or redemptive and divine.

"What comes out of the mouth **proceeds from the heart,** and this defiles (pollutes) a man. **For out of the heart come** evil thoughts, murder, adultery, fornication, theft, false witness, slander. These are what defile (pollute) a man."[27]

Behold, then, the unrivaled service of watchfulness: the regulation of the workshop of the heart with the kinetic energy of Grace and the Name of Jesus. With watchfulness and the Jesus prayer, with neptic prayer, the heart accepts Grace like oxygen, expelling everything impassionate and making our lives exude grace.

WATCHFULNESS
IN DIVINE WORSHIP

Looking carefully at the liturgical wealth of our Church, we note endless points in which watchfulness is mentioned or commented on: in the daily sacred services (Nocturns, Matins, Hours, Vespers, Compline), in the prayers of the Divine Liturgy, in the Great Canon, in the hymnology of the Octoechos, the Triodion, and the Menaia.

The worship of our Orthodox Church is a profoundly contrite worship, a worship of returning into our true, deeper self. In other words, our worship is a neptic worship.

In Nocturns, after Psalm 119,[28] there is a sublime troparion, which is also chanted contritely on Holy Week:

Behold, the Bridegroom comes in the middle of the night; and blessed is the servant whom He shall find **watching,** but unworthy is he whom He shall find in slothfulness. **Beware, then, O my soul,** and be not overcome by sleep, lest thou be given over to death and shut out from the Kingdom. But return to soberness and cry aloud: Holy, holy, holy art Thou, O God: through the Theotokos have mercy upon us.

Immediately after this follows a Doxasticon, also inspired by the parable of the ten virgins:

Keep in mind that fearful day and be vigilant, my soul. Kindle thy lamp and cause it to burn brightly with the oil of compassion. For thou dost not know when thou shalt hear the cry, 'Behold, thy Bridegroom!' **Be watchful,** then, my soul, and **do not slumber,** lest thou be left outside knocking at the door like the five virgins. But continue wakeful, and so with the rich oil of mercy in thy lamp go out to meet Christ thy God; and may He grant to thee the divine bridal chamber of His glory.

In a special service of Nocturns we ask of the Lord, after the evening rest and beginning of the new day, to cleanse us, to make us temples of the Holy Spirit, and to grant us a vigilant heart and a sober mind, so that, no longer asleep in the soul, but awake and alert, we may work His commandments and taste the joy of His divine bridal chamber:

"Almighty Lord . . . grant us to pass the night of the whole present life with wakeful heart **and sober thought. . . ."**

In the third of the twelve mystical prayers of Matins the priest prays on behalf of all the faithful: ". . . Enlighten the eyes of our intelligence that we may never fall asleep unto death in sin. . . ."

In the prayer of the bowing of heads during Vespers the priest prays that the Lord keep us ". . . from every enemy, from every adverse operation of the devil, and from **vain thoughts and evil imaginations."**

In the prayer: "O Thou Who in all times and places . . .", which we regularly read in Nocturns, Hours, Compline, etc., there is a neptic aspect to the phrases, "set our minds aright, cleanse our thoughts."

In the daily evening prayer of the Compline we beseech the Lord for "a watchful mind, a **sober** heart," in other words, alert, filled with vigilance in the spiritual battle with filthy satanic thoughts, which often have their repercussion in our nightly dreams.

Additionally, there are many neptic expressions in the Great Compline. We quote two:

"Enlighten my eyes, O Christ God, lest I sleep to death; lest my enemies say: 'I prevailed over him.'"

We beseech Christ to enlighten the eyes of our soul because a great danger always lies in wait for all fighters: the sleep of death. If he finds us sleeping, the enemy will say maliciously about each one of us: "I prevailed over him — I beat him, I defeated him." And the enemy is vigilant, as another prayer from the Compline states:

"O Lord, Thou knowest well the alertness of mine invisible enemies and the weakness of mine own wretched body, for Thou Thyself hast fashioned me. Wherefore I entrust my soul to Thine hands: cover me with the wings of Thy bounty, **lest I sleep to death;** enlighten my spirit with the delight of Thy divine word; awaken me at the time of Thy glory, for Thou alone art a gracious God and the Lover of Mankind.''

All the ''Hymns of Light'' (Photagogica) which are recited during the Great Lent are known for their neptic content.

*   *   *

There are many and varied degrees and a great variety of pointing ways to watchfulness. We see this also in the Hymns of Repentance in the Octoechos and the Triodion, in which this many-faceted and proper cultivation of neptic life is offered. We note a few to demonstrate this:

> ''Because of all my wicked thoughts and deeds I stand condemned: **put into my heart,** O God, my Savior, **the thought of turning back to Thee,** that I may cry: Save me, loving Benefactor, and have mercy on me.''[29]

> ''Searching my guilty conscience, I cower before Thy fearful Court, O Lord, for my works allow no salvation; but Thou, O Christ God, having a wealth of compassion, have mercy on me and save me.''[30]

Penitential Hymnology constitutes a safe road of return to our lost inner world and always shows us man's only outlet from the immense labyrinths into which he falls, proceeding from searching to anxiety and from anxiety to despair. The only outlet is that of the return of the prodigal. Because, as J. Kornarakis writes, ''whoever goes far away from himself multiplies the inner ruptures and surrenders mercilessly to a disgraceful impasse. The opposite is true, for the one who agrees to enter into his closet, to return to himself, discovers the secret footpath of oneness and harmony of soul and spirit. Furthermore, he views unfathomable and indescribable mysteries, because knowledge of all things is given to him who knows himself; for knowing oneself is the fullness of knowledge of all things.''

21

Here are a few more penitential hymns representative of neptic self-knowledge:

"**When I call to mind** the many evils I have done and **I think upon** the fearful day of judgment, seized with trembling I flee to Thee for refuge, O God Who lovest mankind. Turn not away from me, I beseech Thee, Who alone art free from sin; but before the end comes, **grant compunction** to my humbled soul and save me."[31]

"**Gather together my scattered mind, O Lord, and purify my dry and barren heart,** giving me like Peter repentance, like the Publican sighs of sorrow, and like the Harlot tears, that I may cry with a loud voice unto Thee: Save me, O God, for Thou only art compassionate and lovest mankind."[32]

"Often when I offer praise to God, I am found to be committing sin; **for while I sing the hymns with my tongue, in my soul I ponder evil thoughts.** But through repentance, Christ my God, set right my tongue and soul, and have mercy upon me."[33]

In the third Prayer of Preparation for Holy Communion, we beseech the Lord to come and abide in us in His immaculate Mysteries. We tell Him: ". . . Enter and enlighten **my darkened thought.**"[34] In the Thanksgiving Prayers after Holy Communion we again read: "I thank Thee that Thou hast granted me, unworthy as I am . . . grant that these may be even to me . . . **for the enlightenment of the eyes of my heart** . . . that being kept by them in Thy holiness I may never live for myself but for Thee, our Lord and Benefactor. . . ." In the thanksgiving prayer to the Theotokos: ". . . But do thou who didst bear the true Light enlighten the spiritual eyes of my heart . . . and give me . . . the **recall of my reasoning powers from their captivity."**

After the consecration in the Divine Liturgy of St. John Chrysostom, this prayer follows: "that they[35] may be **unto watchfulness of soul,**[36] unto forgiveness of sins. . . ." Not only before but also after Holy Communion we have need of watchfulness and vigilance toward ourselves. According to St. John Chrysostom, watchfulness of the soul is the first blessed fruit of Holy Communion.

In the Divine Liturgy of the Presanctified Gifts, in the prayer of the second Antiphon, the priest prays: ". . . enlighten the eyes of our hearts unto the knowledge of Thy truth." The enlightenment of the eyes of our heart, in other words, the watchfulness which is given as a divine gift guides us to the thorough knowledge of Divine Truth. The first prayer of the faithful, after a little while, says: "O God, great and praiseworthy, Who by the life-creating death of Thy Christ hast translated us from corruption to incorruption, do Thou free all our senses from deadly passions, setting over them as **a good guide the understanding that is within us.** And let our eyes abstain from evil sight, our hearing be inaccessible to idle words, and our tongue be purged of unseemly speech. Make clean our lips which praise Thee, O Lord; make our hands refrain from base deeds, and to work only that which is well-pleasing to Thee, fortifying our members and minds by Thy grace."

In that most beautiful, deeply neptic prayer we see that all our sensory members and our intellect are secured by the Grace of God: they acquire that spiritual freedom, since this "understanding that is within us" becomes set in our hearts as a "good guide" that attracts Divine Grace and protects the senses.

The second prayer of the faithful next says: "that through them our mental sight may be illumined and we may become children of the light and of the day." With the eye of the mind enlightened by the Immaculate Mysteries, we become children of the light and of the day.

St. Hesychios the Priest makes clear the relationship between Holy Communion and watchfulness by writing:

"When in fear, trembling and unworthiness we are yet permitted to receive the divine, undefiled Mysteries of Christ, our King and our God, we should then display ever greater watchfulness, strictness and guard over our hearts, so that the divine fire, the Body of our Lord Jesus Christ, may consume our sins and stains, great and small. For when that fire enters into us, it at once

23

drives the evil spirits from our heart and remits the sins we have previously committed, leaving the intellect free from the turbulence of wicked thoughts. And if after this, standing at the entrance to our heart, we keep strict watch over the intellect, when we are again permitted to receive those Mysteries the divine Body will illuminate our intellect still more and make it shine like a star."[37]

*   *   *

The great penitential Canon of St. Andrew of Crete conceals within it great neptic wealth. Let's bring to mind some of its precious gems:

"Instead of the visible Eve, I have the Eve of the mind: **the passionate thought in my flesh,** showing me what seems sweet; yet whenever I taste from it, I find it bitter."[38]

"Thou hast heard — **O my soul, be watchful!** — how Ishmael was driven out as the child of a bondwoman. Take heed, lest the same thing happen to thee because of thy lust."[39]

"**Awake,** my soul, consider the actions which thou hast done; **set them before thine eyes,** and let the drops of thy tears fall. With boldness tell Christ of thy deeds and thoughts, and so be justified."[40]

"**Be watchful,** O my soul, be full of courage like Jacob the great Patriarch, that thou mayest acquire action with knowledge, and be named 'Israel,' **'the mind that sees God;'** so shalt thou **reach by contemplation the innermost darkness,** and gain great profit."[41]

"**Rise up** and make war against the passions of the flesh, as Joshua against Amalek, ever gaining the victory over the Gibeonites, thy **deceitful thoughts.**"[42]

"Christ was being tempted; the devil tempted Him, showing Him the stones that they might be made bread. He led Him up into a mountain, to see in an instant all the kingdoms of the world. O my soul, look with fear on what happened; **watch and pray every hour to God.**"[43]

Compunction and watchfulness are united. Whenever there is compunction there is watchfulness also, and whenever the latter is cultivated, the former also blossoms. The watchful soul, the soul that is full of compunction and humility, the soul that "prays to God at all times," unceasingly, becomes "a mind that sees God."

It's worthwhile still to cite the sticheron of Wednesday before Palm Sunday, which is a rare neptic painting:

"Rich in passions, dressed in the deceptive attire of hypocrisy, I delight in the evils of debauchery and immeasurable cruelty by **overlooking my intellect,** lying like another Lazarus before the gate of repentance, starving from lack of anything good and **ailing because of inattentiveness.** But do Thou, O Lord, make me a Lazarus poor in sins, lest I ever fail to obtain the finger that will cool my tongue suffering in the unquenchable fire; but encamp me in the bosom of the Patriarch Abraham, for Thou lovest Mankind."

Many times the agony and the fighting spirit of the watchful fighter become a cry, a sign of alert, a dynamic reveille because "the end draws near." The Kontakion of the Great Canon renders in a most eloquent way the intensity of the neptic being in the watchful sentry of the intellect and heart:

"My soul, O my soul, **rise up! Why art thou sleeping?** The end draws near, and soon thou shalt be troubled. **Watch,** then, that Christ thy God may spare thee, for He is everywhere present and fills all things."[44]

25

WATCHFULNESS:
THE BASIS OF
SPIRITUAL LIFE

It is well known to the neptic Fathers of the Philokalia that three giants of the devil, who demolish the spiritual life of the fighter to its very foundation, are: forgetfulness, ignorance, and indolence. Watchfulness, however, shows itself much stronger than these three treacherous malefactors. It can seize the giants, imprison them, and handcuff them. Because, how is it possible for a watchful Christian, be he monk or layman, to be seized by forgetfulness, in other words, to forget his internal uncleanness, the field of his heart full of public highways and thorny places; how is it possible to forget the Grace of God, which redeems, deifies, restores the distorted human icon to the pristine, divine beauty? How can he forget the heavenly realities, the divine compassion, the incarnation, the proclamation of the Gospel, the crucifixion, the resurrection of the revealed Son of God? How can he forget the Grace and the Love and the Communion with the Holy Trinity? How can he forget the ''hideous mask,'' the past sins, the filth, the realization of which brings pain, contrition, divine humility, compunction? The searchlight of watchfulness illuminates all of these truths, when it enters into the darkest depths of the fighter's personality, and confines the thief of forgetfulness — no matter how gigantic in the commission of evil and destruction he may be.

With the same ease watchfulness captures ignorance in the dangerously underhanded sabotage which it attempts in the camp of the heart. And countless are the damages and infinite the victims it has made with the cooperation of forgetfulness and indolence in a contemporary world which thinks that it knows everything, but ignores the ''one thing which is needful.''[45]

Watchfulness dissolves the darkness of ignorance and with the cooperation and alliance of mental prayer it asks of the Lord knowledge: the knowledge of God (divine knowledge), and the knowledge of ourselves (self-knowledge). Spiritual knowledge is a gift of the Holy Spirit and watchfulness is its forerunner. Without watchfulness and vigilance, ignorance is not recognized, it is camouflaged, it hides, it is full of conceit, especially in the contemporary technological, conceited and arrogant man. And both ignorance and conceit scatter fog and mist. The light of watchfulness reveals the nakedness of both.

With the same strength and effectiveness "mental attentiveness" neutralizes the giant of indolence. It puts negligence to flight, it spurs the soul, it awakens the will, it strengthens its nerves in the working of Christ's Commandments, which is proof of true love in accordance with His word: "If you love Me, keep My commandments."[46]

The Christian can stay free from the bonds of forgetfulness and ignorance, but that is not enough for an awakened conscience. In the spiritual life theory and practice go together. The Christian also is industrious, diligent in the working of the divine Commandments. He is not justified by his works. He knows this perfectly. But he attracts the Grace of God when mental prayer, the unceasing cry of the heart for Divine mercy, like a quintessence, throbs in the remembrance of God, in knowledge and work.

Watchfulness, waylaying the enemies of spiritual life, performs the radically renewing work of self-knowledge upon personal guilt. Without self-knowledge the soul remains immobile and inoperative in the direction of desired purification. Watchfulness eagerly undertakes the work of self-knowledge. Watchfulness and vigilance resemble a drill that advances to the deepest layers of the unconscious, from where, with the beneficent pump of prayer, it will remove its filth, until the clean vein of Divine Grace is found, which from there on will water our entire spiritual existence.

A brother said to Abba Poemen: "My thoughts disturb me, pushing me to put aside my sins and to take notice of my brothers' shortcomings." And the Elder told him about Abba Dioskoros who used to cry in his cell; his disciple sat in another cell. Then when he went to the Elder, he found him crying and said to him: "Why do you weep, Father?" And the Elder answered him: "I weep for my sins." His disciple then said to him: "You don't have any

27

sins, Father." And the Elder answered him: "Know, my child, that if I allow myself to see my sins, three or four more people wouldn't be enough to weep for them."

If we dared to allow ourselves to see our sins, maybe thirty or forty more people would be needed to weep for them. . . .

J. Kornarakis notes: ". . . The lover and embodiment of watchfulness knows that a specific function is appropriate to each of the two sides which work together for the salvation of a soul. Thus the work of the Grace of God is to forgive and redeem, while the work of the ascetic is only to viably attach himself to personal guilt. When he remains steadfast in the viability of this guilt, he does not deny the blessing of Divine Grace. He does not doubt the power of God. He expresses only human weakness and offers to God what he is able to offer, the viability of his guilt. In this way he out-flanks the enemy and attacks him from behind. By this means he lives watchfulness as a psychological, but also a spiritual defensive mechanism which aims at nullifying the ruses of the devil."

*   *   *

Lack of watchfulness causes us not to examine ourselves and the internal, but busy ourselves with others and the external, indeed to be deceived often by seemingly true or imaginary things. Abba Elias related the following from his personal experience:

"It seemed to me that I saw someone secretly placing squash and wine in his bosom. And to shame the demons, positive that it was a mistaken impression, I said to the brother: 'Please, open that up.' He opened then his robe, and it was evident that he didn't have anything hidden in his bosom. I am relating this so that you shouldn't be so sure, even when you see something with your own eyes, or hear something with your own ears. On the contrary," the Father continues, "be attentive to reflections, memories and thoughts, knowing that the sly spirit comes from them to defile the soul and to make it trusting in harmful things, distracting the mind away from our sins and from God."

The neptic, watchful work on our spiritual life will help us evaluate both our acts and our conscience with divine, Biblical criteria.

We read in the Desert Fathers: "Once certain brothers came to Abba Pambo and one of them asked him the following question: 'Abba, if I fast two days and eat two slices of bread, do I save my soul, or am I deluding myself?' And the other one said: 'Abba, if I earn two small coins from my handicraft everyday, and I keep some for my sustenance and give the rest to charity, am I saved or am I lost?'

"Although they begged him a great deal, he did not answer them. After four days they were about to leave. The clergymen consoled them saying: 'Don't worry, brothers, God will reward you. That's the Elder's way: he doesn't speak easily, unless God informs him inwardly.' Therefore, they went to the Elder and said to him: 'Abba, pray for us.' He asked them, 'Do you want to leave?' They answered him, 'Yes.' Then, assuming their acts himself and writing on the ground, said to himself: 'Can Pambo become a monk by fasting two days and eating only two slices of bread? No. Pambo earns two small coins with his handicraft and gives them to charity. Can he become a monk this way? Not yet.' And he said to them: 'The acts are good, of course. But if you don't have your conscience clear in regard to your neighbor, you will not be saved.' And with this information, they left joyfully."

A brother asked Abba Poemen about the influence of thoughts. And the Elder told him: "That problem resembles a man who has fire on his left and a pitcher of water on his right. Then, if the fire ignites, he takes water from the pitcher and puts it out. Fire is the seed of the enemy. Water is to entrust oneself to God."

They used to say about Abba Sisoes of Thebes, that when Church services were over, he would leave for his cell. They used to say: "He is possessed." But he did the work of God, that is the work of watchfulness and prayer.

Once they asked Abba Silouan: "What asceticism did you practice, Father, to receive this wisdom?" And he answered: "I never left a thought in my heart that might anger God."

A certain brother asked Abba Poemen: "Is it better for someone to speak, or to be silent?" The Elder said to him: "Whoever speaks for the sake of God does well. And whoever keeps silent for the sake of God again does well."

Another brother asked Abba Poemen: "How can one avoid slandering his neighbor?" The Elder said to him: "Our brothers and we are two pictures. So, at the time that a man watches and reproaches himself, he sees his brother worthy of honor. But when he seems good to himself, he gazes at his brother as being evil."

*   *   *

Watchfulness, like a general intelligence agency and at the same time the headquarters of military operations, knows how to urgently and unceasingly call upon the omnipotent alliance of divine mercy which immobilizes and disarms every internal and external enemy. But even after this disarmament, it does not rest. It remains the sleepless eye of the soul in its vigilant guard, the never-sleeping observation post, the penetrating searchlight which follows every movement of the world inside the soul, and searches to keep the field of the heart clean, fertile and receptive to the grace and operation of the Holy Spirit.

The purpose of life in Christ is the acquisition of the Holy Spirit, as all the holy Fathers conclude, and as St. Seraphim of Sarov says in his dialogue with Motovilov. But the purpose of watchfulness and prayer is also the same; it coincides perfectly and completely. That is why the faithful who acquire neptic life attain the goal of life in Christ.

Life in Christ is man's mission deified by grace. And the final, ultimate mission of watchfulness and prayer is none other than the theosis of the faithful and the indwelling of the Holy Trinity in the heart, cleansed of demons and passions. How, then, can watchfulness not be one of the most fundamental bases of true spiritual life?

St. Isaac the Syrian very wisely writes: "If we keep the law of watchfulness and the work of discernment in spiritual knowledge, of which life in Christ reaps the fruit, then the struggle with passionate provocations will in no way come near our mind.

"Spiritual richness and the health of the soul are founded in watchfulness and diligence. For as long as one lives, he has need of watchfulness, diligence and vigilance to guard his treasure. If, however, one abandons his post, he will become weak and a victim of robbery.

"You must work spiritually not only until you see the fruit in your soul, but also until your very end. For even ripe fruit is often destroyed by hail."

MENTAL PRAYER
AND OUR SALVATION

"There is salvation in no one else, for there is no other name under heaven given among men by which we must be saved."[47] Jesus is present in His Name as both Savior of all the world and my personal Savior. The Name "Jesus" means "Savior" or "salvation." As I shout the Name of Jesus by itself or with all the words of the prayer, it becomes the link which unites me with the Lord Himself. It opens the road to my salvation and moves my feet to travel on it securely. It brings salvation, that is, Christ within me, Who created me from nothing and is the life and resurrection of my being.

Lev Gillet writes:[48] "Jesus is more than the giver of what we and others need. He is also the gift. He is both giver and gift, containing in Himself all good things. If I hunger He is my food. If I am cold He is my warmth. If I am ill He is my health. If I am persecuted He is my deliverance. If I am impure He becomes my purity. He 'is made unto us . . . righteousness, and sanctification and redemption.'"[49]

*   *   *

All of us want to be saved. We know, however, that for the realization of our salvation two factors work together: the divine and the human, the grace of God and our own will. But we know how distorted and scarred our human nature is, how sick and weak. Many times we intend to go forward, to approach God, to deaden a passion, to implant a virtue in us, and finally we give way. The wings of our will prove to be of wax, our efforts erratic, the foundation of our spiritual substructure rotten. Then, seeing the fragments of human efforts, this saying from the Psalms comes to our lips: "Unless the Lord builds the house, those who build it labor in vain. Unless the Lord watches over the city, the watchman stays awake in vain."[50]

"In vain," then, is every spiritual building, every spiritual guard without the presence of the Lord; consequently, "in vain" every work of ours without prayer. Prayer makes the presence of the Lord alive and changes every work which could have been fruitless into light and glory to the Heavenly Father.

That is why St. John Climacus calls prayer the mother of all virtues. Because prayer gives birth to, nourishes, reinforces and increases every single virtue, every accomplishment of the Christian. "Capture the mother and she will also surrender her children," in other words, the virtues. Only then does our will become victorious, when it unites with divine help.

Unceasingly saying the "Lord Jesus Christ, have mercy on me," you feel in your heart a feeling of omnipotence. It is not unusual, because the power is not yours, but that of Christ Who comes and dwells within you and is grafted into your being. We see this very clearly in St. Paul's saintly life and revealing words: "I can do all things in Him Who strengthens me."[51]

St. Philotheos writes: "The blessed remembrance of God — which is the very presence of Jesus — with a heart full of wrath and a saving animosity against the demons, dissolves all trickeries of thought, plots, argumentation, fantasies, obscure conjectures and, in short, everything with which the destroyer arms himself and which he insolently deploys in his attempt to swallow our souls. When Jesus is invoked, He promptly burns up everything. For our salvation lies in Christ Jesus alone. The Savior Himself made this clear when He said: 'Without Me you can do nothing.'"[52]

We see this also in the case of the Apostle Peter. As long as his gaze was fixed on the person of the Lord, he walked with ease on the waves; he felt no weight. The turning of his mind, memory and love toward Christ, and his dependence on Him had transformed his body. Christ had given him the gift of walking on the sea without sinking.

That attachment of the Apostle, the giving of his soul to the Master, was prayer. As soon as that prayer became weak, his faith weakened at the same time. Hesitations and doubt surrounded him. But even in his fall the lips and heart of the Apostle appeared prayerful. They did not forget the prayer which saved man miraculously: "Lord, save me," he shouted.[53]

33

The Name of Jesus is redeeming when we pronounce it with longing, contrition, and inward sighing.

Gillet writes: "We sinners shall find Our Lord anew at the invocation of His Name. He comes to us at that moment and as we are. He begins again where He has left us or, rather, where we have left Him. . . . In the same manner, when we say 'Jesus' again, after an act of sin or a period of estrangement, He does not require from us long apologies for the past, but He wants us to mix, as before, His Person and His Name with the detail and routine of our life — and to replunge them in the very middle of our existence. . . . If we link the Name with faith in Jesus as propitiation for the sins of all men, we find in the Holy Name the sign of the Redemption extended to all times and to the whole universe. Under this Name we find 'the lamb slain from the foundation of the world,' 'the lamb of God which taketh away the sin of the world.'"[54]

Every second of your life, my brother, can save you or destroy you for ever. For that reason make each second of yours a cry of the Name of Jesus Christ, and make the mercy of the Lord the uninterrupted occupation of your mind. Thus, you seal your salvation in Jesus with a real guarantee for the present and for your eternal future. All creation, all time, all our salvation, all eternity, rely on the mercy of the Lord. When we cry out for that mercy, when we bring it down by the ladder of unceasing prayer, let us then ask God that it may become a mercy of forgiveness, a mercy of repentance, a mercy of purification, the enlightenment of our closed and blind eyes. Without divine mercy each one of us is a hopeless traveler "going down from Jerusalem to Jericho"[55] without the Samaritan, without an Inn. . . . He is a blind man uninformed about the coming and the passing through of Jesus, a blind man who has not yet learned to shout, "Jesus, Son of David, have mercy on me," to shout "all the more," even if demons and people rebuke him to be silent.[56] . . .

"Such being the powerlessness of every human being, what remains possible for the salvation of the soul from the side of human will and strength? Man cannot acquire faith without prayer; the same applies to good works. What, then, is left for him to do?

34

What scope remains for the exercise of his freedom and his strength, so that he may not perish but be saved?"[57]

Who doubts that ascetic and bodily efforts, fasts, vigils, almsgiving, and all good works, will turn out futile in the end, if the heart and mind are not purified? But I do not know how it is possible for the roots of our spiritual being and life to be purified and united with God, unless they are plunged into Christ, and He becomes their sap and nerve, shoot and trunk, flower and fruit.

Holy Scripture tells us man and all creation are involuntarily subject to futility, groaning inwardly as they wait for the liberation of the children of God.[58] Is it not that secret groan of all creation, that inward tendency of every soul toward its God, a form of inner, mental prayer? And man, without realizing it, has this prayer innate in the very depths of his being. That groan, the Christocentric nostalgia, the deep search for Christ, is natural in each one of us. We only need to pull it up from the abyss of our existence like an intact and unexploited treasure.

Of course, God Himself acts in order for this recovery of mental prayer, of the sweetest Name of Jesus, to take place. Prayer is a "gift of Grace," St. Macarios says. But the Lord wants our consent. He is waiting for us to invite Him to act.

THE WHIP
OF JESUS

The spectacle of the Temple with the merchants and the animal bazaar was disrespectful to the sanctity of the place, the situation insulting to God. It was unacceptable to have turned the Temple into a stable, a materialistic center, a money-exchange! It was especially unacceptable to Christ Himself Who saw His Father's house reduced to a house of trade.

> ". . . In the temple He found those who were selling oxen and sheep and pigeons, and the money-changers at their business."[59]

Oxen, sheep, pigeons, etc., with all their offensive odor, their stench, but also with all the filth of their masters, had spread out "in the temple" and had turned it into a regular fair, which justly excused the holy indignation of the Lord.

> ". . . And making a whip of cords, He drove them all, with the sheep and oxen, out of the temple; and He poured out the coins of the money-changers and overturned their tables. And He told those who sold the pigeons, 'Take these things away; you shall not make My Father's house a house of trade.'"[60]

The attitude and actions of Jesus were daring, decisive and brave. Only He could have taken such a stand. Only He could have attacked the impudence of the cattle-dealers and money-changers with courage, frankness and theanthropic authority, without fearing resistance or opposition. He was the "One Who had authority."[61] He was the Master of the House. The Father's house was also His house; the Temple, His Temple also. Its occupation and use by the merchants was not only irreverent and criminal, but also unlawful.

He made a whip and threw out the animals and masters from the enclosure of the Temple. He poured out the coins of the money-changers and overturned their tables. He could not see this sham without acting, without fixing and restoring order and respect.

That is why the prophet had said, "Zeal for Thy house has consumed me."[62] Then His disciples remembered it.[63] Zeal, fire, love, desire, passion for the cleanliness, the propriety of the Temple consumed Christ to His very depth. . . .

We can easily transfer to the spiritual realm this incident of the expulsion of the merchants from the Temple by the imposing presence of the Lord.

The heart of every man is a temple also, a living temple of the Living God. "Do you not know that your body is a temple of the Holy Spirit within you, which you have from God?"[64]

This temple of our heart is built to praise and worship its God and Creator, to throb with love for the Bridegroom "fairer in His beauty than all mortal men."[65] It is created for the Tri-hypostatic God, Father, Son, and Holy Spirit, with His uncreated energies and light, to dwell there.

For this reason a temple, a heart that sparkles with cleanliness and spiritual order is necessary.

The condition of the secret temple within us is often hopeless, even worse than the one the Lord found in the Jewish Temple. The heart is turned into a carnal house of materialistic and demonic business by sly and treacherous merchants: filth, horrible filth, "gibeonite thoughts" rising up from its depths, desires, vices, cupidities, egotism, all types of sin conceived and carried here, "laws at war,"[66] enemies, pirates, corsairs, darkness and chaos.

How, then, will the temple of the heart be cleansed, renewed? How will the beasts with their bestiality, the merchants with their satanic merchandise, leave? And what is that efficacious whip that can bring about this catharsis?

The Name of Christ is the whip because it brings His fearful, dynamic, divine, indomitable presence. It strikes mercilessly at the demons and cleans the stench and filth of the passions. Christ comes into the temple of the heart. He holds a whip; He Himself is also a whip. His Name is also a whip, as is prayer in His Name.

St. John Climacus writes: "Flog your enemies with the Name of Jesus"[67] and "let the remembrance of Jesus be present with each breath."[68]

The Lord does not permit demons to invade the fortress of our soul when we cry out to Christ fervently, with feeling, tirelessly, unceasingly and carefully. And this is a great profit, because the demons are accustomed to secretly teaching wickedness to the soul by means of bad thoughts. And, as St. Diadochos of Photiki says, when the demons enter the heart, they fortify themselves well, and from there they make their war, trying to camouflage themselves and trick us that they are attacking from the outside.

The spiritual fighter, the true Christian, takes from Christ's hands the weapon that is most terrible to the enemies, and advances shouting: "They compassed me about as bees do a honeycomb, but in the name of the Lord I repulsed them."[69]

But there is a difference between the Temple of Solomon and the temple of our heart. What ? There the Lord entered uninvited, voluntarily. Here, in our inner temple, He asks permission. He wants us to open the door and invite Him in. Or rather, to keep inviting Him uninterruptedly, insistently, ardently, unceasingly.

"Zeal for Thy house has consumed me." Do we ever think how great the Lord's zeal and longing is for His house, that is, our heart? Surely it is a zeal a myriad times more intense, a love infinitely more ardent than that which He showed for the cleansing of the Judaic Temple. "Behold," He says, "I stand at the door and knock; if anyone hears My voice and opens the door, I will come in to him. . . ."[70]

JESUS: "ALL THINGS
TO ALL MEN"

Pray unceasingly with the all-powerful Name of Jesus, the sweet Name, the myrrh of heaven. "Thy name is ointment poured forth. They have drawn thee: we will run after thee, for the smell of thine ointments."[71]

Unceasing prayer has a serious practical advantage: the incessant. You can pray unceasingly no matter what you are doing, wherever you are, everywhere and always: at home, at work, on the road, at mealtime, on the bus, on foot, day and night. This prayer insures you a day "holy, perfect, peaceful and sinless." It disperses "the light of Christ"[72] in the path of your life. It perfumes your being with "the fragrance of Christ."[73]

My brother, pray unceasingly. The Name of Jesus makes it worth your while; it blesses your effort, it enlightens the mind, it purifies the heart, it ignites love.

Are you a worker or a merchant? Pray unceasingly. Jesus sanctifies your work, your business. Are you a farmer or a craftsman? Pray unceasingly. Jesus will sanctify your land or your trade. Are you in public school or college? Pray unceasingly. Jesus sanctifies your school or your college. Are you a professional or an employee? Pray unceasingly. Jesus sanctifies your profession or your service. Are you a soldier, immigrant, or seaman? Pray unceasingly. Jesus sanctifies the barracks, the foreign country, seas and oceans. Are you a father or a mother? Pray unceasingly. Jesus sanctifies your household nest. Are you a young man or a young lady? Pray unceasingly. Jesus sanctifies your youth and your visions. He is Eternal Youth. Still, do you happen to be happy? See Jesus with the "prayer." Jesus will perpetuate your joy; He is Divine Joy. Are you sad? Seek Jesus; He is Comfort. Are you desperate? Do struggles and problems plague you? Seek Jesus; He is Hope and Light. Are you sick? Seek Jesus with the "prayer"; He is Health. Are you an orphan or a pauper? Seek Jesus; He is Father, Mother and imperishable Wealth. Are you wise or illiterate? Seek Jesus; He is "the Wisdom from above."[74]

Are you dying? Seek Jesus with the "prayer"; He is the Resurrection and the Life.[75]

St. Symeon of Thessalonica[76] writes: "Let, therefore, every devout Christian say the 'prayer' unceasingly with the mind and lips. . . . Let the priests practice this prayer diligently like an apostolic mission for themselves and their rational flock, just like preaching and the celebration of the holy Sacraments. Let those who live in the world use the prayer as often as they can, because it is the seal and mark of our faith, sanctification, and the opponent of every temptation. All of us, clergy, laity, monastics, must bring Christ to our minds first, as soon as we awake from our sleep. Let us offer to Him the beginning of all our thoughts like a morning sacrifice. It is natural, before anything else, to think of Jesus, Who saved us and Who loves us so much! . . . Indeed, since we call ourselves and are Christians, we have put Him on with holy Baptism, we have been sealed with His holy Chrism, we receive His Body and Blood, we are His members and His temple. . . .

"For this reason let each one make it a rule to have a specific time and number, according to his ability, that he may say the 'prayer' . . . Those who wish for something more can find someone to teach them."

Patriarch Philotheos of Constantinople writes in the Life of St. Gregory of Thessalonica[77] that St. Gregory "had a beloved friend by the name of Job, a very simple but most virtuous man," who could not understand how it was possible for every Christian to pray unceasingly. Speaking with him once the Saint talked to him also about the prayer. He told him that "every Christian in general should strive to pray always, and to pray without ceasing, as the Apostle Paul commands all Christians, 'pray without ceasing,'[78] and as the prophet David says of himself, although he was a king and had to concern himself with his whole kingdom: 'I beheld the Lord ever before me.'[79] That is, in my prayer I always mentally see the Lord before me. St. Gregory the Theologian also teaches all Christians to say God's name in prayer more often than to breathe. . . ." And not only are we to pray, but to teach all others, men, women, and children, the wise and the unlearned, to pray without ceasing. . . .

*   *   *

Our era is characterized by worry, anxiety, neuroses, confusion, the domination of the machine and technology, which press hard upon the life of the heart. Materialism, nihilism, individualism, cruelty, "death of God," death of love, condemnation of spiritual life, absorption by the carnal "I," thirst for worldly knowledge and glory, disdain for spiritual knowledge, forgetfulness of the divine image of man: all these have turned contemporary men into walking question marks moving in an impassable chaos. But if Jesus is the only true peace for all times, He is especially so for our time. Prayer in the Name of Jesus becomes more imperative today. Christ even today proclaims: "My peace I give to you; not as the world gives do I give to you."[80]

If we had made Christ the life of every moment, with unceasing prayer, and if we sought Him incessantly with ardent zeal, then so many hours would not be spent uselessly in vain thoughts, in materialistic conversations and sinful acts, which increase the anxiety and "worldly cares"[81] and remove us from the divine harbor of His peace. People today are unhappy, they have become "nervous wrecks," because they have entered into a life-style which revolves exclusively around their ego and not around Christ. Their path is egocentric, man-oriented, not Christ-oriented. They suffer of psychological disturbances as payment for their scattering of the mind and heart and for wasting their time on the multiple worship of futility. Christ — Redemption — is missing from there. His Name is missing. Missing is the prayer in His Name which restores man to his real track, to his normal path.

Men without Christ suffer a kind of schizophrenia in the heart. In the world there are more unofficial schizophrenics, who circulate in the streets, than those who live officially in the mental institutions.

Unceasing mental prayer makes man avoid the splitting of the personality, find his divine origin, and, searching within himself, discover with inexpressible joy that "the kingdom of God is within us."[82]

41

HOW AND HOW MUCH
TO PRAY

We know people who can walk in the midst of noise and the crowds of Athens, who can walk through Omonoia Square and the most central streets of the capital with their mind undistracted, free, surrendered to unceasing prayer. This means that the prayer brought about in their souls the divine attraction of Christ, the sacred magnetism of Heaven and Heavenly life.

Nikitas Stithatos writes: "He who succeeds in attaining real prayer and floods his being with the love of Christ, does not become a prisoner to his emotions nor does he become attached to anything."

My brother, pray with simplicity and peace, calmly and plainly, like the gentle breeze, like your breath. Only concentrate all your emotions, all your will around the holy Name of the Lord. Let His Name penetrate your soul like a drop of oil saturates a cloth. Surrender all your being and lock it inside His Name.

Yet you will never soften your soul, you will not make it fruitful, fertile, "good soil,"[83] until you teach it to cry and mourn and be contrite before the Cross of the Lord for its sinfulness and for the sins of the whole world, in which it feels it has a share.

Even today there are ascetics, who weep with a universal, life-long lament as they pray for the evil of the world.

*   *   *

Once in a while, before you begin, or during prayer, during a break, and also after fatigue, open the Holy Scripture and take delight in its divine meadows. You will find "green pastures" to "lie down"[84]; you will discover the natural environment your soul seeks. Its hunger and thirst for Christ will be satisfied. Christ is the focal point of Holy Scripture. That is why the prayer of the heart will make you embrace Holy Scripture consuming you with longing for it. And Holy Scripture will again spontaneously return the Name of Christ to your lips and heart.

In order for every prayer to be acceptable to God and bring forth fruit, it must be said with concentration and the gathering of the mind. If you have a lot of concerns in your work, turn your mind to Christ and unceasing prayer, which will give you strength and will guard you so that the "thorns of the cares of the world" will not choke you.[85]

At the appointed hour of the prayer rule "lay aside all life's cares,"[86] and lift up the mind and heart unto the Lord. In order to fly, every bird first rallies around and then centralizes its strength. The greatest success for the cultivation of the prayer of the heart is precisely that concentration of the intellect, the release from every parasite that sucks it dry. We, beginners, need to curb our intellect and force it to stay within itself and occupy itself exclusively with the words of the prayer: "Lord Jesus Christ, Son of God, have mercy on me."

St. Nicodemus the Hagiorite and many Holy Fathers advise the beginners to bow the head and briefly hold the breath as a means of helping the intellect in its self-concentration: LORD JESUS CHRIST — (inhale) — HAVE MERCY ON ME — (exhale).

This can be done for a short time until our intellect is curbed. Later on, let the prayer roll lightly like a stream and, without interruption, water the interior depths of our being. All our attention should be given to the words of the prayer.

Another proven way of saying the "prayer" is to take a deep breath while reciting it five, six, or seven times: "Lord Jesus Christ, have mercy on me. . . ."

In the beginning, as we said, let us force ourselves to say the "prayer" out loud or whispered with a fast cadence, so that the intellect will not have time to form any distracting thoughts. After a considerable time, our intellect will then get used to praying mentally and will become sweetened, as if it had tasted honey. We will want to say the "Lord Jesus Christ . . ." continually, and whenever we break off, the interruption will sadden us.

Our intellect is the "purveyor of the soul." Its task is to take what it sees and hears to the heart, the center of man's spiritual

43

and physical being. Therefore, when we say the "prayer" and do not think about anything else, but pay attention to its words, then while we breathe lightly, the intellect with its own effort and will takes the prayer down to our heart and keeps it there, reciting it rhythmically. This goes on until the Grace of God overshadows our soul. His Grace is the moving force. It moves everything. In the beginning the Grace of the prayer is purifying; afterwards it becomes enlightening. Grace will come after much struggle and effort, tears and mourning, provided we pray wherever we are: walking, lying down, standing up, working, night and day. When the intellect tires, the prayer should be recited orally. When the lips tire, it should be given back to the intellect, until it is filled, saturated. Then the prayer will become energy. In other words, at that time Grace works even without the will of man, when someone may be eating, sleeping, working, or walking, while within him the "prayer" awakens and shouts, flooding him with peace and heavenly joy.

When at last you have prayed sufficiently, according to what you want, you can stop at one or two words of the prayer where your spirit finds rest and your heart is sweetened. For example, let your intellect and lips repeatedly say, "Jesus — Jesus — my Jesus," or "my Lord," slowly and without interruption, with longing that brings tears, with compunction and love.

*　　　*　　　*

St. Basil the Great notes: "An intellect undistracted by external things and not dispersed through the senses among worldly things, returns to itself, and from itself it ascends to God by an unerring path."

We discover the realm of God when the intellect turns and enters the heart. "The Kingdom of God is within us." When man returns unto himself, he feels with uncontained longing the yearning for the pristine beauty which is found in the Name and Person of Jesus Christ.

Every word of the prayer locks inside it a depth of the knowledge and wisdom of God. We can live all of Jesus, all the

Gospels, all the Grace of our Lord Jesus Christ and the love of God the Father and the communion of the Holy Spirit, all the mystery of the world, by means of the Name of the Lord Jesus. Within that cry of the seeking of divine mercy we are conscious of all the grandeur of the Divine Incarnation, the pain of the Fall, and the joy of our Adoption.

The struggle to keep the "prayer" inside our intellect is not only due to its natural weakness and tendency to wander. It also results from the rabid and covert attack of the devil. However, in time our persistence will win. Our mind belongs to God and, little by little, it must become the "mind of Christ."

St. Dionysius the Areopagite calls the return of our intellect to itself and subsequently to the heart unwavering, cyclic. For just as the circumference of a circle returns again to itself and unites, so also the intellect: it returns to itself by means of this cyclic motion and becomes one.

St. Nicodemus the Hagiorite writes: "Once in the heart, do not let your intellect remain idle, but find the indwelling Logos that enables us to think and compose spiritual works, judge and examine inwardly and read entire books without the mouth speaking a word. Once the intellect has found this 'indwelling Logos,' do not allow it to say anything else but the words of the prayer: 'Lord Jesus Christ, have mercy on me.' Just as God transcends all sensible and intelligible things, so must the intellect rise above things perceptible and intelligible in order to unite with God."

Let your will with love adhere completely to the words of the prayer, so that the intellect, the "indwelling Logos" and your will, these three aspects of your soul may become one. Thus, it appears that man is an icon of the Holy Trinity, as St. Gregory Palamas writes: "When the single mind is threefold, while yet remaining single, it is united with the Divine Threefold Oneness, closes the door to delusion and rises above the domination of the flesh, the world, and the prince of this world."[87]

The quantity of prayer depends entirely on our volition. The Holy Fathers write that one cannot practice perfect prayer of the heart without devoting a great deal of time to it.

*　　　*　　　*

How much should we pray, then? **Unceasingly.**
Without interruption. Since the devil, the enemy of our soul,
fights us without ceasing, we too should unceasingly make use of
the fearful and omnipotent weapon of the divine Name.

Since we are in danger of falling into sin every moment and
of grieving the Lord, let us unceasingly repeat His saving Name.
Let us also ask Him for His mercy. St. Diadochos of Photiki says
that when man calls upon the Name of God as frequently as he
can, he does not fall easily into sin.

As long as we desire to find Jesus incessantly within us, let us
call Him unceasingly.

Inasmuch as we want our heart to be ablaze with the incor-
poreal fire of divine love, let us nourish this fire with unceasing
prayer.

As long as we do not want our mind to be imprisoned by vain
and cunning thoughts, let us give it the "loftier thought" of
unceasing prayer. Let this become its "good change," its pleasure,
its delight, its nourishment: the sweeter-than-honey Name of
Jesus.

My brother, frequent repetition and ceaselessness of prayer
will bring you the fruit that you desire. Don't worry if, in spite of
all your effort, you feel internal dryness. Persist. Fruit is the gift of
the Holy Spirit. The Holy Spirit "blows where it wills, and you
hear the sound of it, but you do not know whence it comes or
whither it goes."[88] What God asks of us is to pray, to pray as often
as we breathe.

*　　　*　　　*

It is imperative that we "pursue the prayer" for many years
with a system, with ascesis by forcing ourselves. For our mind is
scattered, diffused, and with difficulty is restrained in the center,
its objective, its happiness which is Jesus. But with time, however,
a blessed day will come when, instead of our "pursuing the
prayer," it will pursue us. It will spring out, it will gush up, it will
overflow from inside the heart, it will charm the mind with the
very delightful name, the "name which is above every name."[89] A

46

blessed time will come then, when although we may be walking, talking, eating, sleeping, the heart will talk to Christ, her adored Bridegroom. "I sleep, but my heart is awake."[90]

Apart from our attempt to pray everywhere and always, under whatever circumstances, it is imperative for us to have daily a designated period in a specific quiet place for regular prayer of the heart. This will be regulated by our spiritual father.

"Frequent practice of [prayer] will teach us attentiveness. Quantity will certainly lead on to quality. 'If you want to learn to do anything whatever well you must do it as often as possible.'"[91]

Indeed. That is how it is. The athlete who wants to succeed in a certain sport struggles, trains and repeats his attempt to improve his performance and to assure victory. The scientist repeats the experiment in his laboratory — even if he fails many times — for a conquest in the field of medicine, technology, etc. The artist repaints the same work many times until he ends with his classic creation.

The same thing happens also with the Christian who wants to become an athlete, craftsman and artist of prayer. He repeats the words of the prayer "LORD JESUS CHRIST . . . HAVE MERCY ON ME." In the beginning with effort, with patience on the untamable mind, but with longing and assurance that he will win his former nature. He will conquer the Name of Jesus, he will imprint it perfectly with the seal of prayer.

Staretz Amvrosii, one of the renowned ascetics of the Russian Church — insisted a great deal on the cultivation of the Jesus Prayer. He had the advice of St. John Climacus as the rule of his life: "Flog your enemies with the name of Jesus; for there is no stronger weapon in heaven or earth."[92] He would relate much to stress the importance of mental prayer. Amongst others, he would tell this impressive story also:

"A certain devout Christian had a myna bird in his house, which he was teaching to speak. The bird also learned the words, 'Lord Jesus Christ, Son of God, have mercy on me,' which that Christian repeated often. One summer day it found the window open and flew out to the street. Then a hawk saw it from on high and rushed toward it. The bird, surprised by the attack, instead of another cry, cried out the prayer, and the hawk — a wonderful thing! — pulled back at once as if someone was chasing it away.

"What do we notice here?" the Staretz concluded. "That, even if the Jesus prayer is said unconsciously, it has its results and makes possible the impossible."

Struggle, therefore, brother, with all your strength to pray without interruption. The more you persist, the faster you will become accustomed to it. The tongue and lips get used to the prayer and, without your realizing it, the companionship of the prayer will become your permanent property. If at some time, for some reason, it stops, you will feel as though you are missing something vital. Your mind will seek Jesus with longing. For frequent prayer creates such a strong habit that will soon become your second nature. That is the goal you must attain.

You cannot be called a Christian, if you do not pray often. All the saints prayed continually and with ardor. Therefore, become a practitioner of unceasing prayer. It will give enlightenment to your mind, because it will always be found underneath and within the enlightening name of Jesus Who is the Sun of Righteousness and the light of the world.

"Truly blessed is the man whose mind and heart are as closely attached to the Jesus Prayer . . . as air to the body or flame to the wax. The sun rising over the earth creates the daylight; and the venerable and holy name of the Lord Jesus; shining continually in the mind, gives birth to countless intellections radiant as the sun."[93]

MENTAL PRAYER
AND THE BEATITUDES

A certain disciple of a great neptic elder used to say that unceasing prayer bestows upon man that blessedness which Christ praises in the Holy Gospel.

It is really like that. Mental prayer makes man "poor in spirit," mournful, meek, hungry and thirsty for holiness, merciful, "pure in heart," peacemaker, blessed in persecution and revilement for the Lord's sake. The Christian who prays with unceasing prayer enjoys this heavenly blessedness. It is the blessedness of Jesus Christ. Because the one who prays with the mind and heart lives the life of Christ and Christ lives in him. "He who abides in me, and I in him, he it is that bears much fruit."[94]

That hermit often remembers the sweet words of his elder and is overcome with compunction. He has the gift of artlessness and innocence. A little old man with white hair, he stands next to you, talks to you, and looks at you with his angelic, child-like figure, full of humility and simplicity.

I stayed a few days one summer in the hut of that elderly hermit. I wanted to rest spiritually, to find myself a little, to breathe the very delightful fragrance of the desert, and to hear something about mental prayer and watchfulness.

The hermitage is quiet, inaccessible to noise, isolated, as are almost all the hermitages of the Holy Mountain. It is buried between two very high, rocky slopes, which form a wild, but tranquil, ravine. Further down, as much as the rocks which reached to the shore opened up for us, we made out the open sea. It was an ideal choice for a hermitage. To the right and left there is no outlet from the rocky mountain slopes; only straight ahead you catch a glimpse of the endless sea. The only broad outlet that your gaze has is towards Heaven. It is an appropriate location for all those who cultivate the prayer of the heart: from the abyss of the ravine to a nostalgic view of Heaven. . . .

One evening, as the sun was setting, we sat in the courtyard on little stools, where I begged him to tell me what his elder had to say about the beatitudes and how he felt as he prayed them.

Even before he spoke to me he got up eagerly and with the agility of a young man, with the unfeigned, simple love which distinguishes the hermits, he cut the best, perhaps the last, grape of the hermitic grapevine and offered it to me with sweet rain water on an old wooden tray.

"First of all, eat these grapes. They are very sweet and ripe."

"And they are twice blessed," I said to him. "They have your blessing, too. They are also the fruit of the desert."

"You see, my child, how each thing comes in its own time. For the ripeness of the grape it was necessary for some time to pass, so that it may give us today the taste and therapeutic beneficial value that it has. The same thing happens with the prayer. My elder used to tell me that one spends many years with patience, asceticism and effort in prayer until he matures so that the soul may render the beautiful fruits of the beatitudes."

"I beg you, Father," I said to him, "to start from the first fruit, 'the poor in spirit' and humility, according to the words of the Lord: 'Blessed are the poor in spirit, for theirs is the Kingdom of Heaven.'"

"May it be blessed. I will tell them to you the way my blessed Elder explained them and lived them. Due to my slothfulness, I was not able to follow him to the height of his views," he said humbly, "neither did I acquire virtue, but I remember his 'my heart has uttered a goodly theme.'[95] This theme of his teaching becomes for me, the slothful, a sentinel who pricks and awakens me to my daily struggle."

I. *The Beatitude of Humility*

"With the searching out of divine mercy," he began to say to me, "we feel ourselves sinful, fallen, beggars, wounded, the lost sheep. And we humble ourselves. We weep and mourn. We remember our sins. We reflect on how much we've embittered our benefactor, Jesus Christ. We resemble the blind man of the Gospel who implored, 'Jesus, Son of David, have mercy on me!'[96] And we ask Him to open the eyes of our soul, to see the light, to see God. The blind man recovered his sight after he took the medicine. What was the medicine? The power of Christ inside the dirt, the spittle, and the pool of Siloam.[97] I believe that our eyes can open, too, with similar medicine. Let us become contrite and humble like dirt, 'dust and ashes.'[98] Let us receive the humiliation of man and demons; this is the 'spittle.' And then, let us bathe in the holy pool of tears. That is what my blessed elder used to say to me.

*   *   *

"It is impossible for true repentance to exist without humility. Besides, how can you be sure that you will be saved without repentance? The very first presupposition of salvation is the conscious, the earnest, complete, and even permanent, constant and unceasing repentance. The tax collector, the prostitute, the thief, the prodigal, the Apostle Peter, confirm this for us. All of them passed through the furnace of repentance, all of them tasted the pain that estrangement from God brings. Thus, they arrived at the joy of salvation, at the delight of the return.

"Therefore, perhaps a more beautiful and more moving prayer of repentance has not been found up to now: 'Lord Jesus Christ, Son of God, have mercy on me.' The continuous and uninterrupted quest for divine mercy transcends even the 50th Psalm,[99] the Psalm of repentance, in depth and power. You surely well up inside with superb thoughts and feelings. But only for a second. Shortly thereafter, they evaporate from your soul. With the prayer of the heart, however, the feeling of poverty and sinfulness begins to become a sleepless way of life, an internal state, which creates a permanent basis of 'ineffable contrition' which makes the soul shrink and tremble from the fear of God, and brings an unceasing repentance in an atmosphere of bright sadness and gladsome mourning." He took the Philokalia in his hands, opened it with respect and read to me the following from St. Hesychios:

"Let us hold fast, therefore, to prayer and humility, for together with watchfulness they act like a burning sword against the demons. If we do this, we shall daily and hourly be able to celebrate a secret festival of joy within our hearts."[100]

"This, then, is the beatitude of humility, of 'the poor in spirit.'"

"So humility later brings joyful mourning?" I asked him.

"Yes, but the opposite also takes place. Gladsome mourning may lead to humility. All of these move in a blessed spiritual cycle."

II. *The Beatitude of Gladsome Mourning*

"Brother, do you want us to cut a bouquet of sweet-smelling flowers from the writings of St. Gregory Palamas?"

"May it be blessed, Father. It would give me great joy, especially since I think that you will talk to me about the gift of prayer called mourning. Joy in mourning then."

"You are justified feeling joy in mourning since it is 'gladsome mourning' and is rightly called so. I'll read and you pay attention." He put on his old glasses and began to read from the Philokalia with such pleasure and absorption, as if he were eating honey. ". . . Non-acquisitiveness is the mother of carefreeness, and carefreeness is the mother of attentiveness and prayer which, in turn, beget mourning and tears. . . . From these spring joy and the blessed laughter of the soul. Then, the bitter tears turn into sweet ones, and the sayings of the Lord become 'sweet to the palate, more sweet than honey to the mouth'[101] . . . the heart learning from these experiences according to the saying, 'O taste and see that the Lord is good;'[102] the delight of the righteous, the joy of the upright, the cheerfulness of the humble, the consolation of them that mourn for His sake.'"[103]

"The first tears of mental prayer are mournful, tears of contrition and pain. Just like the bitter streams from Saint Peter's eyes after the denial in the high priest's courtyard. These tears are tears of repentance. Tears are required in order for the hardness

52

and uncircumcision of our heart to soften and dissolve. 'Raindrops moisten the furrows, and tear-laden sighs rising from the heart soften the soul's state during prayer.'[104]

"For the dry land to be watered and fields to be irrigated a lot of rain and water is necessary. And for the soul to be watered with the Grace of God and to be disposed so that divine states may blossom again within it, tear-soaked sighs are necessary.

"The tears of the 'prayer' have taken something from the ineffable maternal grief and the flame of the fiery sword which tore the heart of our Panagia in front of the Cross. They have taken something from the grateful heart of the leper, from the inextinguishable longing of the beloved disciple of Christ, from the outburst of the joy of the disciples when they saw the Lord 'after He had risen.'[105]

"Mourning turns into unspeakable joy. The tears that unceasing prayer offers are also like those of the publican, contrite, grateful, erotic, resurrectional — and they affect our prayer accordingly: sometimes like the publican's, at times full of divine eros, sometimes filled with the joy of the resurrection. There is no tongue in the world that can express how and why man cries with joy during prayer when he pronounces the name 'Jesus' and what he feels at that heavenly hour.

"When the soul begins to be bathed in tears from the rest and comfort that prayer brings, then the soul itself appears boldly to the Lord and says to Him, 'Let my beloved come down onto his garden, and eat the choicest fruit.'"[106]

"Thank you very much Father, I understand now. Now I feel more clearly the words of our Lord: 'Blessed are they that mourn for they shall be comforted.'"

III.   *The Beatitude of Meekness*

I looked at the very white, ascetic face of the elder. He was silent. His deep-set eyes were dampened by contrition. . . . His gaze now, full of prayer and gratitude, had fallen toward the side of the small cave, between the rocks, where he kept the remains of his revered elder.

I looked at him once more. A cheerful figure full of goodness from whom the beatitude of meekness overflowed. He was able to speak about this through personal experience, since he lived it so earnestly and so naturally.

"Meekness born of mental, unceasing prayer, waters our entire being," he said to me. "And the mercy which God gives to the meek is the mercy of the inheritance of the new earth, in other words, the Kingdom of Heaven. The meek are the luckiest heirs of God, according to the words of our Lord: 'Blessed are the meek for they shall inherit the earth.'"

"How is this beatitude of meekness expressed, Father," I asked him.

"It is not expressed. It is inexpressible experience! However, you can get a glimpse of it through its eloquent silence, its goodness, its unresentfulness, its forbearance, its forgivingness, its cheerfulness."

"How can the soul in prayer which receives the grace of meekness feel?"

"Internally meekness fits in with and takes its strength from the peace of Christ, which spreads its sweet protection with the unceasing invocation of the divine name. 'Gentleness is the substance of humility,' says St. Peter of Damaskos in the Philokalia. Open it and read here where he talks about the second commandment,"[107] he said to me.

I took the Philokalia in my hands and read out loud: "Then, even if someone gets furious with us, we are not troubled —" "He means the meek person," the elder added.

". . . On the contrary, we are glad to have been given an opportunity to profit and to exercise our understanding, recognizing that we would not have been tried in this way were there not some cause for it. Unwittingly or wittingly we must have offended God, or a brother, or someone else, and now we are being given a chance to receive forgiveness for this. For through patient endurance we may be granted forgiveness for many sins. . . . Indeed, nothing leads more swiftly to the forgiveness of sins than this virtue or commandment."[108]

54

"In simple words, he wants to say that the meek man is never disturbed, my brother, but believes that the tempter makes it possible for him to be forgiven, because once he saddened God or his fellow men. Not only doesn't he become disturbed but is happy, reflecting that this opportunity is for him a great spiritual gain. Do you see how meekness, the quickest way for the remission of sins, leads to true joy?"

IV. *The Beatitude of Hunger and Thirst for God*

"Father, permit me to tell it to you the way I feel it. I think that the next beatitude, 'Blessed are those who hunger and thirst for righteousness, for they shall be satisfied,' is not just a fruit of unceasing mental prayer, but also its essence and core."

"Yes, my brother. You are right. You feel a hunger and an unquenchable spiritual thirst when you say the 'Lord Jesus Christ . . . have mercy on me.' Unceasing prayer is itself a gnawing, yet entirely sweet hunger and thirst for our sweetest Savior. Hunger for Him Who is the Food of all the world, the 'Bread of Life.'[109] Thirst for Him Who is the Living Water,[110] the Fountain of Life and Immortality. There were people — and there still exist some — who after being filled with unceasing prayer, felt no material hunger and thirst. 'Man shall not live by bread alone.'[111] My elder, too, was such a man. Then the soul arrives at the point of repeating the words of Christ, 'My food is to do the will of Him Who sent me, and to accomplish His work.'[112]

"Unceasing prayer is the Will of the Father for him who prays. The more he prays, the more he knows God and His mysteries, the more he hungers and thirsts. 'And the more knowledge he gains, the more he thirsts, burning as though drinking flames. And because the Divine cannot be grasped fully by anyone, he continues to thirst for ever,' writes St. Damascene."[113]

"But does he not say that 'they shall be satisfied?' Why does the man who prays remain thirsting?" I asked.

"Hunger and thirst for Christ Who is the only holiness (righteousness) satisfies a man yet does not fill him. It is an insatiable satisfaction. The more you eat and drink of Him, the

55

more you seek Him. The more you enjoy Him, the more you long for Him. Unceasing mental prayer grants this blessed hunger and thirst for the Lord's mercy, for His holiness and grace. Therefore, blessed, most blessed is that Christian who is hungry and thirsty for Christ and prays unceasingly, night and day, in His name.''

V. *The Beatitude of Mercy*

"Just as God is 'compassionate and merciful, long-suffering and plenteous in mercy,'[114] — similar attributes — the same is true with the soul that prays unceasingly. It acquires that beatitude of mercy, not only toward the poor and suffering, but also toward all the people whom it considers brothers, and toward all creation, animate and inanimate.

"According to the words of the Lord, 'Blessed are the merciful, for they shall obtain mercy,' the more our heart becomes merciful, the more it secretly receives divine mercy, which is invoked continually with unceasing pain and longing. 'Lord Jesus . . . have mercy on me.' The more it receives mercy, the more merciful it is. The beatitude of mercy makes our heart broad, large, compassionate and forbearing.''

"When the Lord speaks about mercy and the merciful, does He mean only material mercy, charity?''

"Certainly not only that. You can be merciful to your neighbor even without money. Mercy has a broad meaning; it is a divine embrace of the heart toward every man, which in its extreme limits identifies with love for God and man. 'I desire mercy and not sacrifice,'[115] the Lord commands us in order to show us that above all external and adoring religious expressions of worship, He asks for 'mercy,' love. That love which is not jealous or boastful, not arrogant or rude, does not insist on its own way, it is not irritable or resentful, it does not rejoice at wrong, but rejoices in the right.[116]

"The merciful one never takes material things into account when he is about to be merciful to the image of God, his fellow man. One distributes his money to the poor, another cares for the elderly and sick. Remember the Saint who had picked up a leper

56

from the street and cared for him with unsurpassed patience and self-denial. Another prays with ardent soul, with tears for his brothers. Is there a more authentic expression of mercy than this? Is there a richer mercy than prayer for your neighbor? Therefore, it is enough that love exists in your soul. Then we will be merciful in deed, in word, and simply by our presence. Mental prayer inspires this holy mercy in the heart. Without this, 'our lamps are going out.'[117] And in the end we will hear that terrible 'I do not know you.'"[118]

VI. *The Beatitude of the Purity of Heart*

"My brother, do you know what the most important work of mental prayer is?" the elder surprised me after a brief interruption. "What?" I asked him. "To purify the heart, to achieve the beatitude, 'Blessed are the pure in heart for they shall see God.' All our effort should be directed there."

"Father, in our days we talk about pollution of the environment: pollution in the atmosphere, pollution in the sea, pollution everywhere. But if physical pollution is measurable, the pollution of the contemporary spiritual environment is almost incalculable in breadth and depth. In our days, the prince of this world[119] with the powers of darkness, the demons, have acquired greater influence and contaminating action on mass media, the press, transportation, etc. How can a Christian remain pure in heart in this filthy and polluted environment?"

"My child, I'm not saying," the elder answered calmly, "that the environment does not influence a Christian. But if a Christian is polluted so easily by the external environment, it means that he has not attained internal purification of the heart. That purification is the whole struggle of watchfulness and prayer. The holy fathers say that with the purification of the heart our external senses are also cleansed. And not only that. Pollution is isolated as it attempts to attack and penetrate our inner world. The polluted spiritual air is filtered out by watchfulness and prayer. Therefore, I think you should not worry so much that you live in a polluted environment, as that you have not purified your heart. Many ways were applied and are being applied. One is the surest and most fruitful way for purification: unceasing attentiveness and prayer, Holy Communion and participation in the life of Christ.

"The pure heart stays clean with the Grace of Jesus even in the filthiest environment, like a ray of the sun, like a pearl in mud.

"Remember those holy elders with their spotless heart who for the love of Christ and the salvation of their souls even visited brothels, yet remained dispassionate and unassailable. Remember that saint who looked at the well-groomed woman and cried because he neglected to be presentable to the Lord.

"Remember how the power of attentiveness and prayer rendered the noble Joseph and St. Martinian heroes; how from within the dreadful temptation of the flesh they came out unhurt and with crowns. Remember how St. Anthony remained unassailed to the temptation of gold thanks to attentiveness and prayer. Remember how prayer and attentiveness inspired in myriad ways other saints and saved them from the temptation of ambition.

"The heart supplies blood to all the members of the body, down to the smallest capillary. The same thing occurs in spiritual life. When the heart is free from sin, clean of every passion and of every passionate thought, then all our sensory members will be clean, since they will be supplied by a pure heart.

"St. Symeon the New Theologian writes that the heart is not purified by one or two or ten commandments, but only when all of them together are achieved. But not even then can the heart become pure unless the Holy Spirit enters it. Just as the blacksmith with all his tools can do nothing if fire is missing, the Christian, too, can have all the virtues as tools, but without spiritual fire which cleanses the filth and stench, his heart remains impure."

"Father, which is the greatest impurity for the heart?"

"Pride. 'Every one who is arrogant is an abomination to the Lord.'[120] Isn't that what it says? Then, from it come all the other filth and uncleanness. That is why the humble and broken heart is the purest."

"I would like you to tell me more. Does prayer first purify our intellect or our heart?"

"First it purifies the mind of evil and wicked thoughts. However, with time purification takes place in both simultaneously, because intellect and heart must unite and travel together on the road of the Jesus Prayer. The more the heart becomes purified, the more the intellect becomes enlightened. The more the intellect is purified, the more the heart shines.

"Noxious foods give trouble when taken into the body; but as soon as he feels the pain, the person who has eaten them, can quickly take some emetic and so be unharmed. Similarly, once the intellect that has imbibed evil thoughts senses their bitterness, it can easily expel them and get rid of them completely by means of the Jesus Prayer uttered from the depths of the heart.'[121]

"The power of mental prayer is purifying. No Christian can attain purification of the passions if he does not pray unceasingly and mentally. The 'prayer' purifies the clouds and fog which wicked thoughts create. '. . . And when it is cleansed, the divine light of Jesus cannot but shine in it, unless we are puffed up with self-esteem and delusion, and so are deprived of Jesus' help. For Christ, the paradigm of humility, loathes all such self-inflation.'[122]

"Therefore, when the heart is purified, it arrives at blessed dispassion. As St. Symeon the New Theologian says, with dispassion you see the things of this world, and it is as if you do not see them, because all your mind, all your heart, your feelings and will are absorbed by the Heart and Mind and Will of Christ. But for this to happen, how much struggle, ascetic striving and perseverance are needed on the body and how much persistence in prayer. Until Christ absorbs the soul and our soul absorbs Christ. . . .

"However, my brother, there is no more blessed moment than that in which the Holy Spirit will breathe in the heart with the operation of unceasing mental prayer. The heart leaps, rejoices, delights. All its energies are purified. The final end of both mental prayer and watchfulness is the acquisition of the Holy Spirit. His coming is the most exciting event. The pure heart becomes the temple of the Supersubstantial Trinity, according to the word of God: 'No one can say Jesus is Lord except by the Holy Spirit,'[123] and 'He who loves Me, will be loved by My Father, and We will come to him and make our home with him.'[124]

"How many known and unknown saints have enjoyed the uncreated Taborian light of the Triple Sun of the Godhead on this earth, when the horizon of their souls opened, when the Paraclete, the Spirit of Truth, 'encamped' in them and cleansed them of every 'stain.'

VII.   *The Beatitude of Peace*

"As the heart prays, the mental ears of our soul catch the echo of the divine words: 'Let not your hearts be troubled neither let them be afraid. . . . My peace I give to you.'"[125]

"Father, how can we have this peace? We who live in the world, in a technological world, in a consumer society, with myriad noises, with confusion, haste, anxiety and agonies, quarrels and recriminations, where machines rule in almost everyone of our steps, where rationalism spreads while the soul and spirit retreat at an alarming pace?"

"I think, my brother, that Christ also had in mind our era with the contemporary conditions of the world and life. Unceasing mental prayer can work its great miracle here. The peace of Christ through His Name will spread tranquillity to the mind and heart as it makes the impossible possible and accompanies us on the manifold expressions of our work and occupation, even if around us everyone and everything is shoving and suffocating, and the world finds itself in an endless chase with vanity."

"A great deal of practice of the prayer and spiritual awakening of the mind is necessary, however, for this to be a success."

"Of course. How can we obtain the crown of peace without effort? The inner peace of Christ is a victory over passionate thoughts, whether one lives in the desert or in the crowded world."

"The beatitude says, 'Blessed are the peacemakers.' What does this mean?" I asked.

"When the inner peace of the mind and heart is established, then man becomes a peacemaker. He disseminates peace externally also with his presence, his behavior, his words. He may come up against difficult times, adverse and ill-starred situations, harsh

60

confrontations, disturbed people and demonic temptations. He will face everything and everyone with that peace of Christ which encompasses indomitable courage and great heroism. The peaceful man is a child of God, and his peace is the resurrectional gift of the Risen Jesus. Open the Philokalia and read in the chapters of St. Nikitas Stithatos.''

I opened it and read in the place where the elder showed me: " 'Much peace have they that love Thy law, and for them there is no stumbling-block.' [126] There is much peace in all those who love the law of God and are not scandalized by anything, because everything that is pleasing to man is not always pleasing to God. On the other hand, whatever does not seem good is very good to Him Who knows the nature and principles of all beings and events.''

"I think, my child and brother, that deep peace is born and increases with unceasing prayer. Nothing else nourishes and re-news it as much as the Name of the Lord. Next to that heavenly state of Christ-bearing peace there is patience and the beatitude of persecution and reviling for the sake of the Lord. Many Christians today shudder at persecution and revilement. The saints hoped for it because Christ blesses it. In the so-called Christian society, without Christ, whoever wants to hold onto the Name of Jesus must also keep the yoke of persecution and revilement as a blessing and proof of his true christianity. Mental prayer will give the strength to endure this 'easy yoke.' [127] The Christian is perse-cuted, ridiculed, reviled in countless ways. Mental prayer will disperse fear and cowardice. It will instill in him stalwartness and, most importantly, bliss in this martyrdom of the soul. Finally, from there, the beatitude of joy will emerge. It is the joy of prayer, the joy of God, Who is inside the prayerful heart wholly with His mercy.

VIII. *The Beatitude of Joy*

"Joy, the joy of the Holy Spirit, as His fruit and offspring, is an inalienable, permanent state in the soul which prays unceas-ingly. It is joy 'fulfilled' [128] because it is the joy of Christ which

61

becomes also the joy of His disciples: '. . . that my joy may be in you, and that your joy may be full.'[129]

"We met such men whose faces glowed with the joy of Christ, emitting all around the gladness of Divine Grace! We confirmed that the light of this eternal spring which illuminates these earthly angels is a reflection of their heart praying unceasingly.

"The joy of mental prayer is the resultant of the joy of the whole creation, the joy of the divine Incarnation, of Redemption, of 'the Ascension into Heaven, the Second and Glorious Coming again.'[130]

"Still, the joy of mental prayer is the joy of the Church of Christ (Triumphant and Militant), the joy of the prophets, apostles, martyrs, and ascetics of our faith. The Divine and worshiped Name of Jesus recapitulates everything and everyone, it eternally gives them worth and life. When the Name of Jesus takes root in our mind and heart, then no one will take the joy of Jesus away from us.[131] What the world considers joys are fleeting shadows, refuse, compared to the eternal gain of joy in Christ.[132]

"In order for contemporary man to cover the anxiety and despairing boredom which life without God brings, he perceived a thousand and one joys, replacements, cheap inventions, outbursts of his extroversion which drain him each time more and give him the gall of pleasure to drink. The joy of Christ gives the reward because it is 'full' joy: '. . . so that whatever you ask the Father in my name, He may give it to you. . . . Ask, and you will receive, that your joy may be full.'[133] 'He who through unceasing prayer holds the Lord Jesus within his breast will not tire in following Him, as the Prophet says.[134] Because of Jesus' beauty and sweetness he will not desire what is merely mortal.'"[135]

*   *   *

My discussion with the elder was unforgettable. What I have noted here are but a few of the things he told me, what I kept in my mind. It was late; it was almost midnight. The summer sky flashed with myriads of stars. Absolute stillness reigned

62

everywhere, a symbol of the hermits' undisturbed peaceful soul. The sea allowed its waves, lightly muffled, to play with the pebbles. We sat like that without stirring, both of us mentally praying for a long time, surrendered to the mystery of stillness — out there in the hermitic courtyard, on its wooden seats. My heart was filled with gratitude. I sought to find a message which would tell simply about mental prayer, which could become a right and a gift, not only for monastics, but for all Christians in all the world, so that all the world might be able to live Christ just as those angels on earth called monks live Him with prayer, the unceasing, mental prayer. I allowed its breath to cool me again, to enter into my very depths along with the revered elder, who now had shut his eyes, bent toward his chest breathing rhythmically. He was praying so that he would teach me how to pray. Two tears rolled slowly down his glowing, amber face. . . .

After a little while, he quietly whispered: "However, my brother, there is still another beatitude which I did not tell you. It is the most beautiful, sweetest, most desired of all. Mental prayer guides us there with an insatiable thirst, with a divine intoxication."

I opened my eyes wide and looked at him. "Which one is it, Father?"

" 'He who eats My flesh and drinks My blood abides in Me, and I in him.'[136] Do you understand?"

"I understand, Father. It is the hunger and thirst for the Holy Altar. . . ."

"Go in then. Go to your cell and pray. In an hour I will call you to church to say Matins with the 'prayer.' Then we will celebrate the Divine Liturgy and commune the Heavenly and Priceless Pearl!"

Never before in my life did I ever feel such sweet anticipation. Never before did I enjoy the Divine Liturgy so simply, so deeply. Never before did I enjoy Holy Communion, the Divine, the Eternal Beatitude so strongly . . . there in the poor and humble chapel of the hermitic hut which had been turned into a true king's palace. . . .

THE CROSS
OF THE PRAYER

A pilgrim of the Holy Mountain visited a hermitic skete and stayed in the hut of a known elder. He had the idea that prayer is easy work and that monks do not toil a lot for it. Then the elderly ascetic told him to be obedient and to stay awake one night — according to the typikon of prayer of the hesychasts — and to do prostrations and prayer with the prayer-rope for a certain number of hours.

That man really stayed awake and tried to pray as the elder had instructed him. When dawn finally came, he asked him: "How did it go, brother?"

"What can I tell you, Father. Forgive me. I couldn't wait for daybreak. I feel so tired from the vigil and from the attacks of the evil spirits that I would have preferred to dig in a garden all day with the hoe."

"Brother, the work of prayer, especially of pure prayer, is toilsome. That is why it has so many fruits and gifts."

Indeed. Nothing else can compare with the spiritual fruition of true prayer and no physical toil can compare with the toil of prayer which is accompanied by watchfulness and vigilance. "Incessant prayer within the heart and all that follows beyond this is not reached by simple happening or by short and easy work. . . . It requires long time and much effort and labor both of body and soul, and a long and intense forcing of oneself. . . . St. Barsanuphius says: 'If inner doings with God do not help a man, his external efforts are in vain. For inner doing with a contrite heart brings purity; purity brings true silence of the heart; this silence brings humility; humility prepares man to be the abode of God. . . .' And the great Chrysostom: 'Abide constantly with the name of our Lord Jesus, so that the heart swallows the Lord and the Lord the heart and the two become one. But this work is not done in one or two days; it needs long effort and a long time. For much labor and time are needed before the enemy is cast out and Christ comes to dwell in us.'"[137]

Therefore, as time goes on, brother, and you continue patiently the unceasing work of prayer, a "broken and humbled"[138] publican's prayer, say to the Lord: O Lord, "behold my lowliness and my toil, and forgive my sins."[139] Indeed, great is the glory of prayer, but the toil is great also. A certain saint talks about the "cross of prayer."

He who prays, truly prays, is crucified. He is dead to all the things of this world, his senses, "proper and improper" thoughts, all reasoning. His mind lives the pain and grief of the crucifixion. The prayerful mind accepts the buffetings and spitting of the evil spirits, the crown of thorns of revilement; it is silent with a mystical deathly silence, is nailed on the cross of "kenosis," of "reasonable sacrifice" as accursed, thirsts for divine compassion and love, drinks the gall and vinegar of bitter passions, accepts the absolute abandonment of the Heavenly Father, expires, dies, is buried so it may rise, glorious and victorious in the Grace and glory and Light of the Risen Author of Life.

If the mind does not pass through the cross, it does not arrive at the resurrection. Those who have acquired this experience of prayer crucify themselves, die and rise again. It is an empirical experience of the hymn: "Yesterday I was buried with Thee, O Christ, today I arise with Thee in Thy Resurrection; yesterday I was crucified with Thee; but Thou, O Savior, glorify me in Thy Kingdom."[140] Truly, pure prayer is the Kingdom of Christ.

THE FRUIT
OF MENTAL PRAYER

Why do we pray? Is it for love, longing and divine eros for God, or for the hope of compensation and the wages which the Lord sends with the consolation and sweetness of Grace?

Prayer is a basic necessity of our being as indispensable as breathing. It forms the natural environment of each soul, in which the love for God is the beginning and end. But by no means can we not expect the fruits also, the taste of which makes man more easily attain his divine destination, in other words, his union with Christ, Who is the beginning and source of all good.

*   *   *

St. Makarios of Egypt writes: "When we plant a grapevine, we do it with the thought and purpose of getting grapes. When the grapevine, therefore, does not produce fruit, then all our toils are wasted. That is how it happens in regard to prayer. If we do not aspire for spiritual fruit, in other words, love, peace, joy, and rest, toil for it is pointless. . . ."

The fruits of mental prayer are many and varied, in proportion to the diligence, toil, and purification of each soul, and at the same time, according to how much and in what way, the Grace of God wants to manifest itself to each soul. Divine Grace is attracted by prayer, and when it enters into man it operates in various ways. "The wind blows where it wills, and you hear the sound of it, but you do not know whence it comes or whither it goes."[141] The time and space of the acquisition of Divine Grace is a true paradise. A soul lives dramatic hours afterwards when it is deprived of it due to God's chastisement or its own carelessness.

The presence of the Grace of the Holy Spirit brings divine states, holy gifts, experiences out of this world, ineffable manifestations. The presence of Divine Grace offers man the fruit of the Holy Spirit which "is love, joy, peace, gentleness. . . ."[142] At the same time it grants

— mourning, heartfelt tears, contrition,
— deep exultation of the heart,
— ardor,
— inexpressible enthusiasm,
— understanding of the Holy Scriptures,
— knowledge of the language of all creatures,
— compassion and broadening of the heart for all creatures, for all Nature, animate and inanimate,
— fearlessness,
— purification of passions,
— deliverance from every vanity,
— divine and sweet knowledge through which God is found,
— knowledge of the hidden mysteries of God,
— knowledge and contemplation,
— knowledge and theology,
— knowledge of Divine Love,
— enlightenment of the mind,
— humility, dispassion and discernment,
— participation in the uncreated energies of God,
— light of Divine Effulgence,
— capturing of mind by love and knowledge,
— blessed love, Divine eros,

and a multitude of other divine gifts, spiritual states, and inexpressible, innumerable and unfathomable mysteries.

The Grace of God resembles a mother who appears suddenly, hugs her baby and kisses it. The man who accepts Her like a young child leaps, exults, rejoices, is filled with ineffable sweetness. But when Grace "pulls back," departs, then man cries and laments like an infant, because he does not know the wisdom of God, Who seeks our salvation with understanding, temptations and trials. When the Lord sees that we seek Grace with ardent desire, then He restores Her again. And Grace, like a spiritual mother, gives us the breast of infinite joy and love. And we, her children, now wish to be close to Her forever.

This is how the holy Fathers, who experienced the many-faceted, fragrant breath and gentle breeze of the Holy Spirit, describe the presence of His Grace.

The spirit of delusion has no relation to these states, presents the opposite symptoms, makes the soul fierce, brings disturbance, pride, harshness. We repeat, that is why the spiritual elder is imperative in the holy and unique art of mental prayer.

MENTAL PRAYER
AND DIVINE EROS

The more Jesus takes in your spirit and you take in Jesus, the more inner fervor increases. Love is inflamed. Desire expands. The heart leaps. Jesus is your Creator. He formed you out of nothing. Jesus is your Savior, Friend, Father and Brother. Jesus is your Bridegroom. With the unceasing invocation of His Divine Name you feel that you are already entering His Bridal Chamber, "in the splendor of His Saints."[143] And the more your heart invites Him and lives Him mystically, the more divine Eros wounds it delightfully with His sweet arrows.

The soul enamored with Christ searches with toil and anguish for its Bridegroom until it finds Him. "By night on my bed I sought Him whom I loved; I sought Him but I did not find Him; I called Him but He did not listen to me. I will rise now to search for Him through more strenuous prayer. . . . Perhaps I shall find Him who is present in all things and beyond all things, and feast on the vision of His glory."[144]

This struggle of mental prayer is a struggle of divine eros. It does not leave neither the heart, nor the mind, nor the mouth alone, instead it continually shouts His much desired Name, because love spills out of "all your soul, all your strength, and all your mind."[145] Then man loves the Love that is God and all God's creation. He sees men as images of God and the other creatures as expressions of His divine glory, and weeps for all the world. . . .

The loving disposition of the heart toward Jesus will not allow a second to pass without calling Him, without seeking Him; like the bride who seeks her bridegroom in the Song of Solomon; like John, the friend, virgin and beloved disciple of the Lord, who falls upon the Lord's bosom and stands "by the cross of Jesus;"[146] like the Apostle Paul who preferred to "depart,"[147] to die so that he may live from then on with his Beloved Jesus.

"This warm and attentive prayer, that is, prayer that is pure, gives birth in the heart to desire, to turning towards God and to love towards the ever-remembered Lord Jesus Christ, as is written: 'Thy name is as ointment poured forth, therefore do the virgins love thee;'[148] and: 'I am sick of love.'[149] And St. Maximus says: 'All the virtues assist the mind to turn towards God, but most of all pure prayer; for soaring through prayer to God, the mind is outside all.''[150]

The soul, ''sick with love,'' thirsts for the Lord, and the more it seeks Him the more it loves Him, and the more it loves Him the more it thirsts for Him, and the more it thirsts for Him the more it seeks Him. This love increases. The soul glows. It soars. The mind is captured by divine eros. The heart suffers inexpressible passion: very sweet, tyrannical, delightful, agonizing. The prayer of the divine Name inundates the whole being, it becomes more intense, more dynamic, more alive. It brings the divine presence which is love. The spiritual sense which is the eye of the soul sees everything then, inside and out, heavenly and earthly, visible and invisible, directed by and towards one end: the love of God. He is the Lover and the soul is the beloved who cries out erotic cries like these: ''Thou hast ravished me with longing, O Christ, and with Thy divine love Thou hast changed me.''[151]

''Where are You, Lord? And she persists seeking her beloved Bridegroom, like in the Song of Solomon. She leaves behind all the world to reach the One Who is to be found within the 'cloud of unknowing.' And the soul turns within.

''She withdraws from everything earthly . . . transcends this world . . . strips the mind of fantasies . . . and only by means of the will, having unified her purest powers, with the mind free of form or fantasy, shapes or images, knowledge or intellection, surrenders to her burning desire for God. . . .

''But where is God? Exactly where desire is. Where there is nothing but burning love: 'burning but not consuming'[152] love. The 'vision' of God is there. And in that blazing place the mystical meeting between God, the Lover, and the soul, the beloved, takes place — a meeting transcending human understanding. . . .''[153]

It is impossible for the heart that prays unceasingly not to love God, and it is impossible for the heart that loves God not to pray unceasingly.

Most Christians do not love God anymore. This is our greatest sin, a disaster, a universal calamity. We scattered our love on a thousand and one other things. We fragmented it into infinite loves, countless affairs, vanities and worldly cares, professions, philosophies and arts. Nothing is left now, not even one corner for God. Our heart is filled with everything else; it is empty of divine love. We do not pray because we do not love.

We waste the movements of our mind — thoughts — and the movements of the heart — desires — in manifold deceit, in things external, base. Our Church proclaims: "Let us lift up our hearts."[154] The Apostle cries out: "Set your minds on things that are above, not on things that are on earth."[155] But in vain. We love the world and worldly things. "The world — however — passes away, and the lust of it."[156]

How, then, can we love God, when the mind and heart are so split and scattered? Only with mental prayer and unceasing watchfulness will we unite the "divided" mind and heart and approach God. Because, "when the remembrance of God moves in man's mind, his heart immediately moves toward His love, and many tears flow from his eyes, because love has the habit of bringing up tears when it remembers a loved one."[157]

Then we will be able to experience the Divine Eros in the words of David: "As the hart panteth after the fountains of water, so panteth my soul after Thee, O God. . . . When shall I come, and appear before the face of God?"[158]

FOOTNOTES . . .

[1] St. Thalassios the Libyan, "On Love, Self-control and Life in accordance with the Intellect," Second Century, No. 28, in *Philokalia,* vol. 2, p. 314.

[2] Mt. 7:7.

[3] Jn. 17:3.

[4] Ps. 1:1 - 2.

[5] Ps. 37:14, et al.

[6] Rom. 13:11.

[7] Jn. 14:15.

[8] *The Ladder,* 28:10.

[9] Mt. 25:28.

[10] Mt. 11:12.

[11] Mt. 23:27 - 28.

[12] St. Hesychios the Priest, "On Watchfulness and Holiness," No. 159, in *Philokalia,* vol. 1, p. 190.

[13] Deut. 15:9, LXX.

[14] All scriptural passages are given from the Revised Standard Version (RSV) of the Bible, unless otherwise noted.

[15] Mt. 25:10.

[16] Mt. 25:11 - 12.

[17] St. Mark the Ascetic, "Letter to Nicholas the Solitary," in *Philokalia,* vol. 1, pp. 150 - 151.

[18] Mt. 25:13.

[19] Lk. 21:36.

[20] Mt. 26:41.

[21] Mt. 26:40.

[22] Matthew, chapters 5 - 7.

[23] Mt. 5:28.

[24] Mt. 6:22.

[25] St. Gregory Palamas, *Letter to the Nun Xenia.*

[26] Mt. 23:25 - 26.

[27] Mt. 15:18 - 20.

[28] Ps. 118, LXX.

[29] Aposticha, Tone 1.

[30] Sessional Hymn, Tone 2.

[31] Aposticha, Tone 8.

[32] Aposticha, Tone 3.

[33] Aposticha, Tone 3.

[34] Actually, this quote comes from the Second Prayer by St. John Chrysostom, which, in the Greek usage, is the fourth Prayer in the Service of Preparation.

[35] That is, the Consecrated Gifts.

[36] Here all translations we have seen incorrectly have: "unto cleansing" (nipsin) of souls, rather than "unto watchfulness" (nepsin)!

[37] "Op cit.," No. 101, in *Philokalia,* vol. 1, p. 179.
[38] From the 1st Canticle.
[39] From the 3rd Canticle.
[40] From the 4th Canticle.
[41] From the 4th Canticle.
[42] From the 6th Canticle.
[43] From the 9th Canticle.
[44] Great Canon, Kontakion, Tone 6.
[45] Lk. 10:42.
[46] Jn. 14:15.
[47] Acts 4:12.
[48] *On the Invocation of the Name of Jesus,* p. 10.
[49] I Cor. 1:30.
[50] Ps. 127:1.
[51] Phil. 4:13.
[52] *Philokalia,* vol. 3, p. 25.
[53] Mt. 14:30.
[54] Lev Gillet, *Op. Cit.,* pp. 11 - 12.
[55] Lk. 10:30 ff.
[56] Lk. 18:38 - 39.
[57] *The Way of a Pilgrim and The Pilgrim Continues His Way,* p. 190. Translated by R. M. French, The Seabury Press, New York.
[58] Rom. 8:19 - 21.
[59] Jn. 2:14.
[60] Jn. 2:15 - 16.
[61] Mt. 7:29; Mk. 1:22.
[62] Ps. 69:9.
[63] Jn. 2:17.
[64] I Cor. 6:19.
[65] Holy Saturday, *The Praises,* Stasis I.
[66] Rom. 7:23.
[67] *Ladder,* 21:7.
[68] *Ibid.,* 27:61.
[69] See Ps. 117:12, LXX.
[70] Rev. 3:20.
[71] Song 1:3 - 4, LXX.
[72] Liturgy of the Presanctified Gifts.
[73] II Cor. 2:15.
[74] James 3:17.
[75] Jn. 11:25.
[76] Greek edition of the *Philokalia,* vol. 5, p. 62.
[77] *Early Fathers From the Philokalia,* p. 412 (London, Faber & Faber Ltd.). Cf. also Greek version of the *Philokalia,* vol. 5, p. 107).
[78] I Thess. 5:17.
[79] Ps. 15:8, LXX.

[80] Jn. 14:27.

[81] The reference is to the Cherubic Hymn in the Divine Liturgy.

[82] Lk. 17:21.

[83] Matt. 13:8.

[84] Ps. 23:2.

[85] Matt. 13:22.

[86] Cherubic Hymn.

[87] *On Prayer and Purity of Heart,* ch. 2.

[88] Jn. 3:8.

[89] Phil. 2:9.

[90] Song of Songs 5:2.

[91] *The Way of a Pilgrim,* p. 209.

[92] *Ladder,* 21:7.

[93] St. Hesychios the Priest, "Op. Cit.," No. 196, in *Philokalia,* vol. I, p. 197.

[94] John 15:5.

[95] Ps. 45:1.

[96] Mk. 10:47.

[97] Jn. 9:6 - 7; see also Mk. 8:23.

[98] Gen. 18:27; Job 30:19.

[99] The allusion is to psalm 51, or 50th, according to the LXX. The super-scription to the Psalm reads, in part: "A Psalm of David, when Nathan the prophet came to him, after he had gone in to Bathsheba." It is the penitential Psalm par excellence.

[100] *Philokalia,* vol. I, p. 193, #176.

[101] Ps. 118:103, LXX.

[102] Ps. 33:9, LXX.

[103] St. Gregory Palamas, Letter to Nun Xenia.

[104] Ilias the Presbyter, in *Philokalia,* vol. 3, No. 106, p. 61.

[105] Mark 16:14.

[106] Song of Songs 4:16.

[107] *Philokalia,* vol. 3, p. 96.

[108] *Ibid,* vol. 3, p. 95.

[109] John 6:35, 48.

[110] John 4:10.

[111] Deut. 8:3; Mt. 4:4.

[112] John 4:34.

[113] *Philokalia,* vol. 3, p. 96.

[114] Ps. 144:8, LXX.

[115] Hos. 6:6; Mt. 9:13, 12:7.

[116] I Cor. 13:4 - 7.

[117] Mt. 25:8.

[118] Mt. 25:12.

[119] Jn. 12:31; 14:30; 16:11.

[120] Prov. 16:5.

[121] *Philokalia,* vol. 1, p. 196, #188.

[122] *Ibid.,* vol. 1, p. 193, #175.
[123] I Cor. 12:3.
[124] John 14:21, 23.
[125] John 14:27.
[126] Ps. 118:165, LXX.
[127] Mt. 11:30.
[128] Jn. 17:13.
[129] Jn. 15:11.
[130] *The Divine Liturgy,* mystical prayer before the consecration of the Holy Gifts.
[131] Cf. Jn. 16:22.
[132] Cf. Phil. 3:8.
[133] Jn. 15:16; 16:24.
[134] Cf. Jer. 17:16, LXX.
[135] *Philokalia,* vol. 1, p. 188, #148.
[136] Jn. 6:56.
[137] SS. Callistus and Ignatius Xanthopoulos, "Directions to Hesychasts," ch. 52, in *Writings From the Philokalia On the Prayer of the Heart,* pp. 227 - 228.
[138] Ps. 50:17, LXX.
[139] Ps. 24:18, LXX.
[140] Paschal Canon of Matins, Third Ode.
[141] Jn. 3:8.
[142] Gal. 5:22 - 23.
[143] Prayers of Preparation for Communion.
[144] Ilias the Presbyter, "A Gnomic Anthology," Part IV, No. 94, in *Philokalia,* vol. 3, p. 59.
[145] Lk. 10:27.
[146] Jn 19:25.
[147] Phil. 1:23.
[148] Song 1:3.
[149] Song 2:5.
[150] SS. Callistus and Ignatius, "Directions to Hesychasts" in *Writings from the Philokalia on the Prayer of the Heart,* p. 231.
[151] Prayers of Preparation for Communion.
[152] Ex. 3:2.
[153] Theokletos Dionysiates, *The Theology of Mental Prayer* (in Greek).
[154] The Divine Liturgy.
[155] Col. 3:2.
[156] I Jn. 2:17.
[157] St. Isaac the Syrian.
[158] Ps. 41:2, LXX.

RECOMMENDED READINGS

1. St. Hesychios the Priest, "On Watchfulness and Holiness," in *Philokalia,* (London & Boston, Faber & Faber, 1979), vol. I, pp. 162 - 198.

2. Nicephorus the Solitary, "A Most Profitable Discourse on Sobriety and the Guarding of the Heart," in *Writings from the Philokalia on Prayer of the Heart,* (London, Faber & Faber, 1971) pp. 22 - 34.

3. St. Gregory Palamas, "On Prayer and Purity of Heart: Three Chapters," in *Early Fathers from the Philokalia,* (London, Faber & Faber, 1969) pp. 409 - 411.

4. The Blessed Callistus Patriarch, "Texts on Prayer," in *Writings from the Philokalia on Prayer of the Heart,* (London, Faber & Faber, 1971), pp. 271 - 273.